MANAGING AND GROWING
GOD'S RESOURCES

Copyright © 2009 by STEVE MAIN

All rights reserved. The use of any part of this publication reproduced, transmitted in any form or by any means, electronic, mechanical, photocopying, recording, or otherwise, or stored in a retrieval system, without the prior written consent of the author – is an infringement of the copyright laws of the United States of America.

All scripture quotations, unless otherwise indicated are taken from the HOLY BIBLE, NEW INTERNATIONAL VERSION® NIV® Copyright © 1973, 1978, 1984 by International Bible Society. Used by permission of Zondervan.
All rights reserved.

ISBN 978-0-9818691-4-8

Book Cover and Design by Amanda Humphrey

Editing by Eric Novak, Modern Media Perspectives

Printed in the United States of America

Published by The Changing Point Carson City, Nevada

www.stevemain.com

Contents

1. **Forward**
   by Ian Hill

4. **In Memory of**
   Pastor Dick Johnson

7. **Introduction**
   Discipline, God First, Neighbor Next, The Sheep and the Goats, Attitude Counts

34. **I Laying The Ground Work For Management**
    One Master, Money Influence, Fear, Greed, Tithe, What to count

58. **II Letting Go and Surrender To God**
    Faith, Trust God, Thankfulness, Thorn in the flesh

74. **III Managing and Growing Resources**
     Content Point, The Budget Formula, Getting Out of Debt, Investing, Debt, Economy, Setting up A Brokerage Account

118. **IV Engaging And Serving God**
     Prayer, God's dimensions, The Value of Labor, Home Maker, Pastor, Missionary, The Great Commission, Rich vs. Poor, Rest in the Lord

Forward
by Ian Hill

" All In " is a poker term for betting all that you have and it has come to mean giving your all to something.

In my life I have literally met thousands of people and if there is one who stands out as an "All in" kind of person, its Steve Main, and in his case "All in" refers to his walk with God.

I have watched and experienced Steve and his love for the Lord. It shows itself in his obedience to God's teachings, in his serving of others and in the way he handles all the resources that God has given him which are time, talent and treasure.

If you ask Steve how he managed to achieve all of his success and his wealth, he will flat out tell you that it is all because of God.

To say that Steve is a success is somewhat of an understatement for he has built many things out of nothing. He built an athletic career at both the high school and college level out of very little except heart and determination. He built a successful business out of savvy and hard work and he has built a financial philosophy that has helped many through studying and his common sense approach. What is constant in all these examples and through everything in Steve's life is his complete reliance on God to show him the way. Whether it be to provide his strength or to guide his path, Steve gives full acknowledgement that God

> Read it carefully and then pray, pray some more and then read it again

alone deserves the glory for everything that he has accomplished.

If you ask Steve how he managed to achieve all of his success and his wealth, he will flat out tell you that it is all because of God. In fact he would likely add that "I actually have nothing for it all belongs to God and I just manage some of it for him."

Is Steve a saint? No...what man is? (His wife Laura, on the other hand certainly is, but not Steve). He is flawed like the rest of us, but what sets Steve apart, and why I believe he has God's favor in his life is because he is "All in" for Jesus Christ.

I would humbly suggest that when reading this book you take an "All in" approach as well. Read it with the belief that God is going to do something special through it and through you. Pay attention to what he writes in the book - read it carefully and then pray, pray some more and then read it again. Let the words on the page seep into you heart and let it provoke Holy thought. In your time of prayer ask God "What do you want me to see in this book" and most importantly ask in prayer "What do you want me to do because of what I have read?" Just reading this book and then setting it down to go about your life as you were doing before hand will be a complete waste of your time and a glorious opportunity lost.

If you aspire to be a great steward of what God has given you; if you want Him to entrust you with more than what you currently have, then you must read and learn from these pages. Remember that learning has not occurred unless one's behavior has changed which is why I'm telling you to act immediately upon what you will read in this book.

We can gain through Steve Main not only Godly principles on financial management but we can also learn a more important lesson. We can learn that in God's economy whoever is willing to be "All in" are those that God will call upon. If you have any doubts about this, just look at Steve.

Father, may those who read this book be blessed. May it be the tool that they use to profoundly change their lives, and may that change bring you glory and honor. Holy Father I also ask that you bless Steve Main for his obedience, humble service and for giving his whole heart to you.

In Jesus name I ask,

Amen

IAN HILL

IN MEMORY OF
PASTOR DICK JOHNSON

DICK JOHNSON reminded me of the apostle Paul. I always have and always will call him Mr. Johnson. That is how I will address him in heaven unless I am not allowed to. He always said, "Call me Dick". I never did. Not only did he finish the race well, he ran a long race and did not trip during that race. I cannot give Mr. Johnson credit for his service to others and to God while he was here. He would not take it anyway. I have to say, I stand in awe of what God can do in someone's life who really loves Jesus.

I often wonder why did I have the privilege of having Mr. Johnson teach me and mentor me as a young child? Why didn't everyone have the same opportunity? Mr. Johnson was my Sunday school teacher. He taught me about all the kings of Israel. I know about all the stories in the Old Testament because he taught them when I was in grade school. He challenged kids in his class to memorize scripture, invite friends to Sunday School, show up, and bring their Bible. I did all those things every Sunday because the reward was a trip to an amusement park or a Major League Baseball game. I thank God for the blessings He has put in my life. Dick Johnson was truly one of these blessings here on Earth.

This book is about budgeting the resources which God has given us. The resources we have under our management can touch one life, and that can impact the world. When our labor is committed to God, it will multiply in ways we

> I always have and always will call him Mr. Johnson

do not see at present. Our labor can multiply for many generations. It's kind of funny when I think about Mr. Johnson's influence. Not only did I bring a friend to Sunday School every Sunday, I made sure they memorized their Bible verse and brought their Bible because I wanted them to go to the Giants/Dodgers game with me. As a little boy, my motives were kind of selfish. Guess what? Mr. Johnson knew that and was wise to it. Even my selfishness got other little kids saved. I know that for a fact since these kids know the same stories I know.

When I think of Dick Johnson, I say, "Thank you, Jesus" for he has heard the words, "Well done, good and faithful servant". Mr. Johnson was an athlete and a competitor who loved sports. Now he has received the grand prize which is eternity with Jesus Christ. I cannot wait to see him again. Right now he is visiting with many of the people he taught me about. I can picture the look on his face since right now he is a kid in a candy store. He might be having dinner with Moses tonight. I say visiting with many because some of the people he taught me about do not have the luxury of being where he is. Many people will not receive this luxury because they don't understand what the Word of God says and what pleases Him. Many people described in the Bible are not enjoying the presence of Jesus because they didn't receive His gift.

His wife Carolyn and his children, Brenna and Scott, are blessed. I know their joy is indescribable and their personal loss is not permanent.

INTRODUCTION

Managing and Growing God's Resources is a book which will lay out some exciting strategies for developing a Godly budget that will begin to grow for His glory. I believe that these strategies will help to eliminate fear and greed, which are two of the forces that can prevent Christ's followers from reaching their God made potential. For those of you who have read "A God Made Millionaire", we will delve deeper into some of the concepts from that book. We will address "the poor mentality" by exposing some of its lies and disguises. We will evaluate the value of labor and the spiritual implications of its multiplication or lack thereof. Most importantly, we will establish a "Content Point" and anchor it on the Rock. This "Content Point", which will be discussed later, will help to shift our focus off of the world and onto "The Great Commission".

> When we do not help others in need we are leaving Jesus cold and hungry

"Then Jesus came to them and said, "All authority in heaven and on earth has been given to me. Therefore go and make disciples of all nations, baptizing them in the name of the Father and of the Son and of the Holy Spirit, and teaching them to obey everything I have commanded you. And surely I am with you always, to the very end of the age." (Matthew 28:18-20).

The budget we create must establish a Content Point and develop a method of helping others in need. When we help others in need we are actually giving to Christ. When we do not help others in need we are leaving Jesus cold and hungry.

DISCIPLINE

Many in the United States have become lazy, self-indulgent gluttons who are devoid of any form of discipline. Many people seek a quick fix for the lusts of their flesh, fears, and desires. Doctors do not hesitate to prescribe drugs for almost anything regardless of need, and our culture gobbles them up in order to fix depression, anxiety, or whatever acronym identified condition they or their children have been loosely diagnosed with.

It seems to have become a contest between trendy restaurants to see which one can pile the most food on a plate. These plates seem to get bigger every year. A family of four is served enough food to sustain a family of twelve. I fear that our country has become nothing but a country full of idols. All a person has to do is follow their fear, greed, selfishness, and anxiety to the end of the trail and they will find the hidden idol. It needs to be said here that just because someone is a believer in Christ does not mean that they are following and serving Him. Even demons believe in Christ.

In order to develop and follow a budget with God's resources and talents, a person must

> Many in the American culture have become lazy, self-indulgent gluttons devoid of all discipline.

expose and eliminate the hidden idols in their life. We must also maintain at least some form of discipline. Discipline is required when we budget any of our resources whether it is our time, talents, labor, or stored labor in the form of money or other assets. It will be easier for an individual who has sold out for God to have discipline.

Many people often live for the moment and spend what they have on their pleasures. However, the key to a successful budget is to have the discipline to be able to live under ones own means. What this means is that a person spends less each month than the income coming in each month. We cannot spend more time or money than what is allocated to us. Anyone can make this choice but it does take discipline to maintain this choice every day. The choices that we make to be responsible with the resources God has put under our management is a choice to serve Him as opposed to our lusts and idols that are in our lives.

"If anyone comes to me and does not hate his father and mother, his wife and children, his brothers and sisters—yes, even his own life—he cannot be my disciple. And anyone who does not carry his cross and follow me cannot be my disciple."

"Suppose one of you wants to build a tower. Will he not first sit down and estimate the cost to see if he has enough money to complete it? For if he lays the foundation and is not able to finish it, everyone who sees it will ridicule him, saying, 'This fellow began to build and was not able to finish.'"

> "Or suppose a king is about to go to war against another king. Will he not first sit down and consider whether he is able with ten thousand men to oppose the one coming against him with twenty thousand? If he is not able, he will send a delegation while the other is still a long way off and will ask for terms of peace. In the same way, any of you who does not give up everything he has cannot be my disciple.
>
> "Salt is good, but if it loses its saltiness, how can it be made salty again? It is fit neither for the soil nor for the manure pile; it is thrown out."
>
> "He who has ears to hear, let him hear" (Luke 14:26-35).

If we love God and our neighbor, everything else will fall into place

Serving Jesus is serious business. He calls us to give up all that we have. We must evaluate the cost. God does not want us to take the decision of following Him lightly. The decision to become a disciple of Christ should be a complete commitment, not a partial commitment.

GOD FIRST

If we love God and our neighbor, everything else will fall into place. If we love God we will love our neighbor.

> "Teacher, which is the greatest commandment in the Law?" Jesus replied, "Love the Lord your God with all your heart and with all your soul and with all your mind." This is the first and greatest commandment. And the second is like it,

love your neighbor as yourself." "All the Law and the Prophets hang on these two commandments" (Matthew 22:36-40).

> God wants us to put Him first. He does not want or need our leftovers

Our Father in heaven gave us an example. He gave us His first and He gave us His best. He gave us His Son Jesus Christ. This sacrifice has given us everything. His first and only Son redeemed the rest of us. I believe God wants us to give first and to always give our best.

Cain and Abel both brought an offering to the Lord. Why did God look on Abel's offering favorably but Cain's offering unfavorably? Cain brought his offering out of his abundance just like the rich people in Luke chapter 21.

"As he looked up, Jesus saw the rich putting their gifts into the temple treasury. He also saw a poor widow put in two very small copper coins. 'I tell you the truth,' He said, "This poor widow has put in more than all the others. All these people gave their gifts out of their wealth; but she out of her poverty put in all she had to live on." (Luke 21:1-4).

Cain waited to bring an offering of his fruits of the soil. Cain brought an offering out of his abundance. He was not trusting God to take care of his future. He trusted in what he had accumulated. He also did not give God his best. Abel, however, gave God the best of his increase and he also gave God the first of his increase. Abel trusted God to provide for his future. He knew that

God had given him what he had and God controlled what would come in the future. He knew that God would give him an increase on his offering. Abel demonstrated his faith through his offering.

> *"By faith Abel offered God a better sacrifice than Cain did. By faith he was commended as a righteous man when God spoke well of his offerings. And by faith he still speaks, even though he is dead"* (Hebrews 11:4).

Read the following passage carefully and the difference between Cain and Abel's offerings should be clear.

> *"'Now Abel kept flocks, and Cain worked the soil. In the course of time Cain brought some of the fruits of the soil as an offering to the Lord. But Abel brought fat portions from some of the firstborn of his flock. The Lord looked with favor on Abel and his offering, but on Cain and his offering he did not look with favor'"* (Genesis 4:2-5).

God wants us to put Him first. He does not want or need our leftovers. This is not because He is selfish, but because He wants us to demonstrate our faith and where our heart lies. God does not need us. Instead, it's we who need Him. God has proven that He is not selfish.

In 1 Kings Chapter 17, Elijah was hiding from his enemies. God ordered the ravens to bring Elijah food. In time the brook Elijah was drinking from dried up, because there was to be no rain except at Elijah's word.

God then told Elijah to go to Zarephath where a widow would give him food. One slight problem was that this widow did not have food. However, nothing is a problem for God. He will take care of us just like He promises. Here is what happened:

"As surely as the Lord your God lives," she replied, "I don't have any bread—only a handful of flour in a jar and a little oil in a jug. I am gathering a few sticks to take home and make a meal for myself and my son, that we may eat it—and die."

Elijah said to her, "Don't be afraid. Go home and do as you have said. But first make a small cake of bread for me from what you have and bring it to me, and then make something for yourself and your son. For this is what the Lord, the God of Israel, says, "The jar of flour will not be used up and the jug of oil will not run dry until the day the Lord gives rain on the land."

She went away and did as Elijah had told her. So there was food every day for Elijah and for the woman and her family. For the jar of flour was not used up, and the jug of oil did not run dry, in keeping with the word of the Lord spoken by Elijah (1 Kings 17:12-16).

This widow trusted God and did what He wanted her to do first with her limited resources. When we trust God, He takes care of the rest.

All authority in Heaven and Earth belongs to Jesus. Everything belongs to Him regardless of whether we know it or acknowledge it. All of the resources He has put under our management should be used for what pleases Him. He owns it all.

> *"The silver is mine and the gold is mine," declares the Lord Almighty"*
> *(Haggai 2:8).*

NEIGHBOR NEXT

If we love God and our neighbor, everything else will fall into place. If we love our neighbor we love God.

I spent some time unbeknownst to the readers of "A God Made Millionaire" discussing some behaviors of people close to me. One person who was not unaware is my wife Laura. She took offense to my comment that she shops at inexpensive clothing stores for herself. I'm sure the readers knew I was complimenting her, but it sure did put me in the dog house. She said, "Now you did it. I can't go outside of the house. You didn't just say inexpensive clothing stores, you said very inexpensive. Why did you have to use the word very? It wouldn't have been so bad if you had just said inexpensive. Now you have to take me shopping."

Let me tell you about my wife. She is probably the most unselfish person I know. Those who know us know that we spend quite a bit of time at Lake Tahoe. In late

January, we spent a week up at the Lake. It was very cold. It was so cold we couldn't spend much time outside with the kids.

We decided to venture out, so we all got bundled up with only our cheeks showing. We walked across the village to a very small candy shop next to an ice skating rink. Laura said to the kids that they could have one piece of candy. Our kids are like all others. They like candy, but they feel that they do not get it often enough because Laura makes sure they eat healthy.

Since I do not carry cash, I handed the young lady working in the store a credit card, however she advised me that the credit card machine was broken. Surprised, I said "You must be losing a lot of business." Laura had struck up a conversation with this young lady as she always tends to do. During the conversation we found out that she had three jobs and all were in the village. Our kids were not going to miss out on this rare opportunity for candy so I walked over to a movie theater on the other side of the skating rink to get some cash out of an ATM machine in order to pay the lady. After we left the store, Laura said to me "I have to buy her a coat". I thought to myself, "Why, was I that rude?" You see, Laura always takes an interest in others. She found out that this young lady had kids, but had no car, and no coat. She walked to work every day in the chilling cold. Wow! "The King will reply, 'I tell you the truth, whatever you did for one of the least of these brothers of mine, you did for me.'" What an honor to serve the King.

In the end, Laura bought a very nice coat and took it to the lady. Laura then explained to her that Jesus wanted her to have it. He does not want anyone to be cold. Have you ever seen that blank look on a speechless person? Well that is what I saw at that very moment and I have to admit that it's pretty cool. It is a look of shock, joy, thankfulness, and surprise all rolled into one.

THE SHEEP AND THE GOATS

"When the Son of Man comes in his glory, and all the angels with him, he will sit on his throne in heavenly glory. All the nations will be gathered before him, and he will separate the people one from another as a shepherd separates the sheep from the goats. He will put the sheep on his right and the goats on his left.

"Then the King will say to those on his right, 'Come, you who are blessed by my Father; take your inheritance, the kingdom prepared for you since the creation of the world. For I was hungry and you gave me something to eat, I was thirsty and you gave me something to drink, I was a stranger and you invited me in, I needed clothes and you clothed me, I was sick and you looked after me, I was in prison and you came to visit me.'

"Then the righteous will answer him, 'Lord, when did we see you hungry and feed you, or thirsty and give you something to drink? When did we see you a stranger and invite you in or needing clothes and clothe you? When did we see you sick or in prison and go to visit you?"

> When we see people in need, we see Jesus in need.

"The King will reply, 'I tell you the truth, whatever you did for one of the least of these brothers of mine, you did for me.'

"Then he will say to those on his left, 'Depart from me, you who are cursed, into the eternal fire prepared for the devil and his angels. For I was hungry and you gave me nothing to eat, I was thirsty and you gave me nothing to drink, I was a stranger and you did not invite me in, I needed clothes and you did not clothe me, I was sick and in prison and you did not look after me.'

"They also will answer, "Lord, when did we see you hungry or thirsty or a stranger or needing clothes or sick or in prison and did not help you?"

"He will reply, "I tell you the truth, whatever you did not do for one of the least of these, you did not do for me.'

"Then they will go away to eternal punishment, but the righteous to eternal life."
(Matthew 25:31-46).

This passage should really strike a chord with Christians. How often do we see or hear of someone in need and then do nothing?

That is why we are here. We are here to find Jesus, and to help Him. These opportunities are all around us every day and they are just waiting for us to discover them. We should not be so caught up in our own selfishness that we fail to pay attention to others and miss these wonderful opportunities. That is exactly why we want to manage the resources that God gives us. That is why my beautiful wife does not often buy expensive clothing for herself.

> People who want more stuff have a poor mindset because they do not have enough

God wants us to put others before ourselves. Jesus uses a parable in Matthew 20 to demonstrate that being first is not always an advantage. A landowner hired men early in the morning to work in his vineyard. The first men were hired for the day and agreed to work for a denarius. The land owner went out four more times throughout the day and each time hired others to work in his vineyard. At the end of the day, he called the workers hired last and paid them first. The workers hired first were paid last. All the workers were paid a denarius no matter how long they worked. "So the last will be first, and the first will be last" (Matthew 20:16). Jesus said the people who will be great are the ones who serve others.

> *"Whoever wants to become great among you must be your servant, and whoever wants to be first must be your slave—just as the Son of Man did not come to be served, but to serve, and to give his life as a ransom for many." (Matthew 20:26-28).*

I have to admire and praise my sister in-law, Kevann Lamkin, for her wisdom in helping those in need. She is an unselfish prayer warrior which is certainly appreciated by my immediate family. She is committed to praying for my daughter Kamryn's and my son Dawson's future spouses. She prays that God will bring them together according to His will. I admire intercessory prayer warriors like Kevann. She has a passion for praying for others.

Something Kevann does for people in need is something that we all can do without enabling people. She has a ready pack of food in her car for when she sees homeless people holding up one of those signs "Will work for food". Of course what the sign sometimes actually means is "Will work for alcohol or drugs but I don't really want to work and I just want you to give me money for alcohol or drugs". If we hand them money, we are handing them what they do not need. Kevann hands them food, which is what they do need.

When we see people in need, we see Jesus in need. Since we love Him, we should also help Him and rack up some treasure in heaven. The Bible says to put our treasure in heaven not hoard earthly treasure here.

Kevann's husband, my brother-in-law, is an unselfish Professor at Azusa Pacific. Although Kevann would disagree with me at times, if you knew what he gets paid you would agree with me. Bryan has a passion for teaching history in a Christian environment. He could make a lot more somewhere else, but he is following God's vision for his life and using his labor for the glory of God. He is putting others before himself. We will never know what the value of his labor is until we see his reward.

ATTITUDE COUNTS

We must all understand that we are all in situations because of the choices we have made.

In "A God Made Millionaire" I discuss behaviors and ways of thinking. I wrote about the "haves", the "have-nots", a "wealthy mindset", and a "poor mindset". I use these terms to describe attitudes. When I use these terms, they have absolutely nothing to do with how many material possessions or how much money a person has or lacks. There are people with a lot of "stuff" who have a "poor mindset". You can be certain that the reverse is also true as there are people with less stuff who have a "wealthy mindset". People who want more stuff have a poor mindset because they do not have enough. Simply put, people who have a poor mindset are not content. Those with a "wealthy mindset" trust God while those with a "poor mindset" do not. The "have-nots" make excuses for their situation and they blame everything and everyone including those people they see as the "haves". The "have-nots" think they are owed something from others; they think the "haves" are lucky. Ultimately, people with a "poor mindset" have an entitlement attitude. The "have-nots" have a tendency to "white-knuckle" their money because they are afraid that they don't have enough or that they might lose it. They say things like, "money is not important". However, if this was really the case they wouldn't be holding on to what they have so tightly. The "have-nots" are takers and fearful while the "haves" are givers and rich toward God.

People with what I call the "poor mindset" or the "have-nots", don't understand what money is or what the value of labor is. Also, they are not acting on what God says. Unfortunately, the American culture, behaviors and ideals are beginning to change. In many ways they are shifting toward the "poor mindset".

It seems that our public schools and universities are spewing more and more propaganda nonsense every year. The main stream media is twisting facts and taking information out of context in order to promote their agenda. Much of today's news is not factual information. It is just someone's opinion. Sadly, the public is swallowing all of this hook, line and sinker. We are spoiled by the abundance that flows in this country. This is happening because Americans are being "dummied up" by being taught political opinions instead of reading, writing, science, and math through the school system. Many parents have turned their children into spoiled brats by giving them whatever they want just to shut them up. Training a child to know right and wrong and to give them a foundation for a future is harder than just giving them what they want. Many of my readers know that I often use television commercials to clarify my ideas. I recently observed a commercial in the form of a duet between a father and his son. This hefty kid, who is at least eighteen years old is asking daddy for a cell phone. Why is this grown man asking dad for a phone? Even worse, dad gives in and tells junior he can have the phone. I'm pretty certain that this ad never would have worked in the fifties. The grown kid sings back that he will love dad forever. What is going on here?! It seems to me that we are breeding a lot of people with an entitlement attitude and it is not even being noticed. Even if this kid was ten, he could figure out how to earn enough money to buy his own phone.

I believe that many educators are teaching students their own political views instead of educating them objectively on facts as opposed to opinions. I feel that many university students are being completely brainwashed by their equally brainwashed professors. I have a feeling there are not many kids being taught that they are responsible for their choices, behaviors, and their own situations. We must all understand that we are all in situations because of the choices we have made. Some people do have it better or worse, but our choices do make a difference. It is not someone else's fault or responsibility.

Many politicians make statements that would only make sense to a person with an entitlement viewpoint. There seems to be a movement sweeping our country which is just a disguise for socialism. People with the "poor mentality" advocate wealth redistribution and government hand-outs. These beliefs and this way of thinking is a Socialist mask. Poor-minded people do not realize they think with a Socialist mind set, yet that's what they do. They are taught to rely on others and that they are entitled to receive certain things. Empowerment is a trait that the poor are seldom taught It seems to me that socialism contributes to the "poor mentality" and causes people with this mindset to think they deserve something they don't.

It is my personal belief that wealth redistributors repeat the same lies over and over until those with the "poor mentality" begin to repeat them causing the public to accept them as facts. Here is what dictionary.com has to say about Socialism;

"A theory or system of social organization that advocates the vesting of the ownership and control of the means of production and distribution, of capital, land, etc., in the community as a whole."
"(In Marxist theory) the stage following capitalism in the transition of a society to communism, characterized by the imperfect implementation of collectivist principles."
(http://dictionary.reference.com/browse/socialism)

If we want a fair tax, everyone would pay the same percentage

Here are typical statements we have heard many times from politicians: "We must increase taxes on the "haves". The wealthiest people are not paying their fair share. They have more than they need."

In "A God Made Millionaire", we studied the parable Jesus told of the talents. Let's revisit it here and evaluate it a little deeper. Try to absorb the principles Jesus is teaching in this parable. We can learn a lot from this parable:

"Again, it will be like a man going on a journey, who called his servants and entrusted his property to them. To one he gave five talents of money, to another two talents, and to another one talent, each according to his ability. Then he went on his journey. The man who had received the five talents went at once and put his money to work and gained five more. So also, the one with the two talents gained two more. But the man who had received the one talent went off, dug a hole in the ground and hid his master's money.

"After a long time the master of those servants returned and settled accounts with them. The man who had received the five talents brought the other five. "Master," he said, "You entrusted me with five talents. See, I have gained five more."

"His master replied, 'Well done, good and faithful servant! You have been faithful with a few things;

I will put you in charge of many things. Come and share your master's happiness!"

"The man with the two talents also came. "Master," he said, "You entrusted me with two talents; see, I have gained two more."

"His master replied, 'Well done, good and faithful servant! You have been faithful with a few things; I will put you in charge of many things. Come and share your master's happiness!"

Then the man who had received the one talent came. "Master," he said, 'I knew that you are a hard man, harvesting where you have not sown and gathering where you have not scattered seed. So I was afraid and went out and hid your talent in the ground. See, here is what belongs to you."

"His master replied, "You wicked, lazy servant! So you knew that I harvest where I have not sown and gather where I have not scattered seed? Well then, you should have put my money on deposit with the bankers, so that when I returned I would have received it back with interest."

"Take the talent from him and give it to the one who has the ten talents. For everyone who has will be given more and he will have an abundance. Whoever does not have, even what he has will be taken from him. And throw that worthless servant outside, into the darkness, where there will be weeping and gnashing of teeth'" (Matthew 25:14-30).

> Let me tell you what tax breaks are: They are business expenses.

Since the master was pleased with the first and second servants for increasing

> I have found nothing in the Word of God that says the government should manage our talents.

wealth and managing what they had been given well, he put them in charge of more. Why wouldn't he? The first two servants increased the resources the master gave them. I believe God wants us to use all gifts, talents, and resources He has given us to take the gospel to the world and make disciples.

Because the last servant was fearful, he did nothing with what the master had given him. He knew the master expected growth, but the servant was afraid of failure. What a wimp.

The master was angry with the last servant and penalized him. The master took what the last servant had and gave it to the first servant who had the most. The master said "Everyone who has will be given more, and he will have abundance". The first two servants were good stewards of what the master gave them to manage. The wicked, lazy servant was thrown into darkness.

People with the "poor mentality" think that money is green air. Let's look at some of the ways they think. They think that the "haves" are hogging up all of the green air. The "haves" are breathing up all of the green air and leaving nothing for the "have-nots". On top of this, the "haves" are causing global warming with all the green carbon monoxide they are exhaling and killing polar bears. This sounds stupid because it is. God controls the climate, not people.

Poor minded people think the first servant is not entitled to what he increased. Socialists believe, the first servant is entitled to nothing more than the last servant. The first servant must give the increase to the last servant.. In order to do this, they must adjust the tax structure because they are sick of politics that don't take talents from the "haves" who increase resources and give to the "have-nots" who do nothing with them. Is this what the parable Jesus told teaches? Socialists think the rules should be changed because people who earn money are keeping some of it.

How did our culture get to a point where so many people think they deserve something that someone else has earned?

Here is why socialists do not think people who earn a lot of money are paying their fair share. A married couple in the highest tax bracket pays a 35% tax rate after deductions. Their exemptions have been removed because they make too much money. If this married couple earns $1 million a year they will pay almost $350,000 just in federal income tax. This is not counting state income taxes and social security. When it is all said and done this couple could be paying half of their income in taxes. Of course this is not fair. This couple should pay at least $750,000 per year because $250,000 is plenty of green air for them to breathe. As a matter of fact letting them keep $250,000 is still hoggish.

Socialists claim people who make less money are paying more taxes than people who make more money. Of course they are. A married couple with net earnings of $63,700 per year in 2007 pays $8,772.50. This is less than 15% of their income in federal income tax. As a matter of fact, this couple actually made about $80,000 per year. Their standard deductions and exemptions bring their taxable income down to $63,700. Anyone who has watched the news even once or has graduated from an Ivy League school knows $8,772 is a lot more than $350,000. It does not take a rocket scientist to know 15% is higher than 35%. A couple earning about $18,000 per year will basically pay nothing in federal income tax. Everyone knows nothing is more than something. Yes, I am being sarcastic, but this is what socialists and people with the "poor mentality" expect us to believe. Recent tax cuts lowered the lowest tax bracket from 15% to 10%. This is a 33% reduction. The highest tax bracket was cut from 39% to 35% which is not much. Only someone with a poor mentality would think the tax cuts were for the rich. If we want a fair tax, everyone would pay the same percentage. If we want a tax cut for the rich, which is what the parable of the talents advocates, they would pay 5% and the lowest income earners would pay 10%. Even with this tax structure people making $1 million a year would pay $50,000 which is more than what the lowest income earners would pay. People earning $50,000 would pay $5,000 which is ten times less than the high earner.

Of course a socialist (redistributors of wealth) would accuse me of applying fuzzy math because they expect me to be stupid and believe that people who occupy the lowest tax bracket must pay social security like everyone else. Hey, that is not fair! The problem with this argument is that social security is paid back many times over in social security benefits to the person who paid it. Of course, the people who earn the most are carrying this burden through their businesses and paychecks. Small business owners pay about 15% to social security. This is called self- employment tax. What is shocking is that this same small business owner makes half of their employees' social security payments as well. The employee pays half and his or her employer pays the other half for them. On top of this, the business owner pays half of an employee's Medicare. The business owner also pays for unemployment and all kinds of other business taxes. They are paying for almost everything. Why are these facts never mentioned by politicians? A more amazing observation is why more people are not articulating this in any effective manner.

The next complaint coming from socialists is that the "haves" get all the tax breaks so they are not paying taxes on their gross income. Let me tell you what tax breaks are: They are business expenses. Business expenses pay for jobs. Socialists do have a way to eliminate business investment and tax deductions. It is called the Alternative Minimum Tax (AMT). Do some research on it. If this is not eliminated, it will just be a matter of time before even the lowest income earners are handing over most of their paycheck to the socialists. By the way, I have found nothing in the Word of God that says the government should manage our talents. The bible says we should give our talents to God/the church and that is how wealth should be shared.

The bottom line is that socialists want to reward people who have the "Poor mentality" and are ineffective with their own talents as well as penalize the first servant who has multiplied his own talents. This is not the principle Jesus was teaching in His parable. It is the reverse. Jesus was not teaching wealth re-distribution. He did not advocate taking talents that the first servant had multiplied and giving them to the third.

How would a socialist or someone with a poor mentality address the three servants in the parable Jesus told? It would be opposite of how the master in Jesus' parable addressed the three servants. What would a socialist say to the third servant? It would sound something like this: "You poor little frightened servant; you have so many excuses for your irresponsibility. You were dealt a bad hand. You have every reason to be a cry baby. I will tell you what I am going to do. Just to be fair, I am going to take all the talents from the two wicked, selfish, green air-hogging servants and give them all to you because you deserve it. It's not your fault they are lucky. All I ask is that you vote for me to remain the master so I can continue to take talents from those who have them.

I'll spend some of them and give you some until we squander them all and there is none left."

So what is my point? My point is, do not fall into the poor mentality trap. If you have a poor mentality, get rid of it. The first servant did not get lucky and the last servant was not unlucky. The last servant did not use his talent. The first servant owes the last servant nothing. I believe God has given us ALL talents and a purpose.

As I stated earlier, people with the "poor mentality" think they are owed something. They think they deserve what someone else has. How did our culture get to a point where so many people think they deserve something that someone else has earned? Politicians and even television commercials often say, "You deserve it". I say, as a believer in Christ, it's a good thing that I don't get what I deserve. We deserve worse than nothing, yet through Christ we receive everything.

Socialists also have many people convinced that if they don't have health insurance, someone should give it to them. Socialists tell people, "If you don't have enough money, we will take it from people who have more than they need and give it to you". This is not what the parable of the talents teaches us. For the readers of "A God Made Millionaire" once again, what does need have to do with anything?

Please note that the master just put the first two servants in charge of many things. He put more resources under their management. The socialist's attempt to redistribute assets is futile. No matter how hard the socialists try to take from the first two servants and give it to the fearful poor minded servant, it will not work. God is the one who will decide who is in charge of His assets and He does not lie.

Isn't it interesting that the people earning $1 million a year are the ones paying for almost everything? That is right; they are the "haves" and the givers.

People in a disadvantaged position often need a hand up. It is my goal to help those people without enabling them. We must first trust God by losing the "poor mindset" and becoming "haves" no matter how much we have. We need to stop making excuses and start being thankful. We can all be "haves". God will do what He says He will do.

The "have-nots" with a "poor mindset" can become "haves" with a "wealthy mindset" simply by changing where they put their trust. When we put 100% of our trust in God and nothing else, we become "haves" with a "wealthy mindset". When people put all their trust in God, they will not blame others or anything else for the situation they are in. The "haves" do not think people or the government owe them anything.

I. LAYING THE GROUND WORK FOR MANAGEMENT

STARTING POINT

The third servant in the parable of the talents could have doubled his talent just like the first and second servants. If he had done this, he likewise would have been praised like the first two servants. If the first servant had buried the five talents the master gave him to manage, he would have been reprimanded also.

I believe that just because someone has little, it does not mean they aren't givers with a wealthy mindset. There are also people with much who are takers. Percentages work the same way for giving just as they do in the tax structure and also for the widow in Luke 21:1-4. A person with $100 who gives $20 gives ten times as much as someone with $10 million who gives $200,000. This is exciting! People with less can easily give more than people with much. I am sick of hearing about wealthy people who give less than one percent of their wealth to the poor. They do not care about the poor. They care about themselves. They care about how they look to others and about making themselves feel good. The people giving large dollar amounts are the ones who often get the attention from men, but

> I believe that just because someone has little, it does not mean they aren't givers with a wealthy mindset.

> We can all be "haves" no matter how much we have.

God notices the ones who give the bigger portion of resources they have under their management.

The good news is God owns everything and He never applies fuzzy math. No matter how hard some people try to change God's rules, they cannot and they never will. The "haves" are givers whereas the people who have the "poor mindset" are takers. Here is what God says:

> *"Give, and it will be given to you. A good measure, pressed down, shaken together and running over, will be poured into your lap. For with the measure you use, it will be measured to you."*
> *(Luke 6:38).*

It doesn't matter how much someone has or doesn't have. Anyone can be a giver and help others. No matter how much each of us has, I believe it's most important not to have a "poor mindset". God has plans to prosper us. It does not matter where we start; God is the one who redistributes wealth. We can all be "haves" no matter how much we have. It is important to remember that we are just the managers of God's wealth.

> *"A good man leaves an inheritance for his children's children, but a sinner's wealth is stored up for the righteous"*
> *(Proverbs 13:22).*

God says if we are faithful with little, we will also be faithful with much. If our heart is right and we are good stewards of what we have, we can be trusted with true riches.

"Whoever can be trusted with very little can also be trusted with much, and whoever is dishonest with very little will also be dishonest with much. So if you have not been trustworthy in handling worldly wealth, who will trust you with true riches? And if you have not been trustworthy with someone else's property, who will give you property of your own? (Luke 16:10-12)

This is very exciting! We can all be good stewards and responsible with what God has given us. Some people aren't born into an advantaged position; however this doesn't matter for disadvantage will be transformed into advantage when God's principles are applied.

I have to state that I was not born with a silver spoon in my mouth and I still do not have one in my mouth. I started tithing when I was about ten years old. I put myself through college on a monthly budget of about $350. My parents gave me something far greater than money. They taught me about Jesus and biblical principles. My parents followed biblical-financial principles and they taught me to do the same. They told me when I was a young boy that if I wanted to go to college, I better figure out how to do it. I will tell my children the same thing. If God wants them to go to college in a particular state, He will make a way. If I feel like He is telling me to pay with His money, I will.

I do think it's important for all of us to realize that we don't know what it's like to live in cultures other than our own.

> I think my mother's favorite two words together are "trust God".

Growing up I always had food, clothing, and a roof over my head. I do know what it's like when the cupboards are empty during those last couple days of the month. I did not grow up in luxury in the eyes of the world, yet in my eyes we had vast luxury. I don't know what it's like to be born into wealth or into poverty. I do think it's important for all of us to realize that we don't know what it's like to live in cultures other than our own. That also includes the different cultures within the United States. We don't always know how others feel and what their unique challenges are. We are often quick to judge and slow to listen. We all need to do more than just listen. We need to hear. I do know our God is bigger than any situation we are in and His word is true.

My Dad is a very hard worker, although he does not work that hard anymore. My parents raised five children on a teacher's salary. My dad was a high school teacher and coach. He also did tax returns, umpired baseball and softball games, cut wood in the summer, kept score for basketball games and sold walnuts from our yard. He left the house very early and came home well into the evening many days. From this, I learned to be a hard worker at an early age. My siblings and I were the ones who picked up and shelled the walnuts my dad sold. I was with him cutting wood. I was with him and I watched him work. I was also on the bus traveling with whatever team he was coaching.

My childhood home was full of love and my parents are huge givers of all that they have, including their time. As I look back on my childhood, I remember a comment I made to my mother years later: "Mom, we grew up in a fairy-tale land". She said, "No, we didn't Steve. We had problems like everyone else." I said, "Like what, our dog Tippy died at age twenty-three". God even blessed our dog. My sister Cindy, who is two years younger than me, knew that dog from the time she was born until she was twenty-two years old. It was hard to believe, but the dog was older than my sister. God always took care of us and provided abundance for us. I know that this might be hard for most people to believe, but my parents never had an argument. I asked my mother years later if she and dad have ever agued. She said, "no but we have had disagreements". That's not a fairy-tale, that's just plain weird. Now my parents' worldly possessions include a motor home they travel in, the stuff in it, and a small car they tow behind the motor home. When I see my parents, I see the same thing everyone sees: Joy bubbling out of them. You have to get out of the way of this gushing joy or it will engulf you and put you in my parents' strange happy place. I think my mother's favorite two words together are "trust God". Anyone can have this.

God does not show favoritism! If we act on biblical principles, God will do what He says.

> Even though racism and unfair judgments abound, we are all equally important to God.

> "Then Peter began to speak: 'I now realize how true it is that God does not show favoritism but accepts men from every nation who fear him and do what is right'" (Acts 10:34-35).

In order for us to have complete financial freedom, the influence of money must be removed from our lives

Yes, some people are born in countries mired in poverty. Some people are born into very poor neighborhoods. Some people are born with extreme disabilities. Some children do not have parents or anyone on earth who show them love. Come to Jesus and be rich with abundance. It does not matter what our race is or skin color. God loves all children.

> "But if anyone causes one of these little ones who believe in me to sin, it would be better for him to have a large millstone hung around his neck and to be drowned in the depths of the sea" (Matthew 18:6).

We are all His children.

> *"For you created my inmost being; you knit me together in my mother's womb.*
>
> *I praise you because I am fearfully and wonderfully made; your works are wonderful, I know that full well.*
>
> *My frame was not hidden from you when I was made in the secret place.*
>
> *When I was woven together in the depths of the earth, Your eyes saw my unformed body.*

All the days ordained for me were written in your book before one of them came to be"
(Psalm 139:13-16).

Although it's tempting to use our culture or environment as an excuse, please do not do this! Even though racism and unfair judgments abound, we are all equally important to God. Do not put God in a box. Realize that nothing is too big or hard for God to overcome and that the grass is not greener on the other side of the fence. We should all be excited about who God made us because he made each of us special and unique. We all have talents and a purpose and each of us can do something that no one else can do. Do not think that people with a lot of money are in an advantaged position. They are not. As a personal trainer in Palm Springs California, this was very obvious to me. I saw some of the richest people in the world who had to be more miserable than the poorest people in the world. The more money many of them had, the worse off they were. It does not take money to be happy. As a matter of fact, money can make people extremely miserable. Money can bring ruin.

I know that God can do anything. If we trust Him and our heart is right, He can make the poorest person in the world the manager of billions of dollars. That money is going to serve the King if our heart is right. We must start with being responsible and good stewards of what God has given us. If we are good stewards, He will increase our resources. We need to be stewards of our talents, money, stuff, and time no matter how much of each we have.

ONE MASTER

In order for us to have complete financial freedom, the influence of money must be removed from our lives. The fear of not having enough and the greed of wanting more must be overcome. We must trust God in our financial situation and be content in that situation. Only then we can focus on truly serving Him.

> *"No servant can serve two masters. Either he will hate the one and love the other, or he will be devoted to the one and despise the other. You cannot serve both God and Money."*
> *(Luke 16:13).*

People who love money and are eager for it have made it an idol in their lives. If we are going to serve God, we cannot serve money. Anyone is capable of serving money even if they have little.

> *"For the love of money is a root of all kinds of evil. Some people, eager for money, have wandered from the faith and pierced themselves with many griefs"*
> *(1 Timothy 6:10).*

Jesus met a wealthy man, who asked him what he needed to do in order to inherit eternal life. Jesus later told His disciples that it is harder for the rich to enter the Kingdom of God than it is for a camel to go through the eye of a needle. Here is what happened:

"As Jesus started on his way, a man ran up to him and fell on his knees before him. "Good teacher," he asked, "what must I do to inherit eternal life?"

"Why do you call me good?" Jesus answered. "No one is good—except God alone. You know the commandments, "Do not murder, do not commit adultery, do not steal, do not give false testimony, do not defraud, honor your father and mother.""

"Teacher," he declared, "all these I have kept since I was a boy."

Jesus looked at him and loved him. "One thing you lack," He said. "Go, sell everything you have and give to the poor, and you will have treasure in heaven. Then come, follow me."

At this the man's face fell. He went away sad, because he had great wealth.

Jesus looked around and said to his disciples, "How hard it is for the rich to enter the kingdom of God!"

The disciples were amazed at his words. But Jesus said again, "Children, how hard it is to enter the kingdom of God! It is easier for a camel to go through the eye of a needle than for a rich man to enter the kingdom of God."

The disciples were even more amazed, and said to each other, "Who then can be saved?"

> Jesus said it's harder for a rich man to enter the Kingdom of God than it is for a camel to go through the eye of a needle.

> Godliness is not a means to financial gain.

> *Jesus looked at them and said, "With man this is impossible, but not with God; all things are possible with God."*
>
> *Peter said to him, "We have left everything to follow you!"*
>
> *"I tell you the truth," Jesus replied, "No one who has left home or brothers or sisters or mother or father or children or fields for me and the gospel will fail to receive a hundred times as much in this present age (homes, brothers, sisters, mothers, children and fields—and with them, persecutions) and in the age to come, eternal life (Mark 10:17-30).*

Jesus told this man that no one is good except God. This man basically ignored that comment and proceeded to tell Jesus how he was good by keeping the commandments. I am going to go out on a limb here and make a guess. This man, ironically, gave a false testimony. His god was money, not Jehovah. He followed the laws of money, not God's laws.

Jesus said it's harder for a rich man to enter the Kingdom of God than it is for a camel to go through the eye of a needle. This statement amazed the disciples of Jesus. I have heard a number of theological explanations on what Jesus meant by a camel going through the eye of a needle. I will discuss what I believe the principle is that Jesus is teaching here. I believe the disciples might have been mixing worldly success with spiritual success.

"If anyone teaches false doctrines and does not agree to the sound instruction of our Lord Jesus Christ and to godly teaching, he is conceited and understands nothing. He has an unhealthy interest in controversies and quarrels about words that result in envy, strife, malicious talk, evil suspicions and constant friction between men of corrupt mind, who have been robbed of the truth and who think that godliness is a means to financial gain" (1 Timothy 6:3-5).

> Do we use our money and things to increase the resources we have under-management for God's glory and purpose?

In the time of Jesus and shortly thereafter, people like the Pharisees and Sadducees were teaching rules for the sake of their tradition. They piled rules on top of rules in the hope that this would benefit them. These rules must have influenced the disciples of Jesus to some degree or He would not have warned them of these teachings.

"These people honor me with their lips, but their hearts are far from me. They worship me in vain; their teachings are but rules taught by men" (Matthew 15:8-9).

"...'be on your guard against the yeast of the Pharisees and Sadducees.'" Then they understood that he was not telling them to guard against the yeast used in bread, but against the teaching of the Pharisees and Sadducees" (Matthew 16:11-12).

Someone must have been teaching that godliness was a means for financial gain. Godliness is not a means to financial gain. Paul says in 1Timothy that only people of corrupt minds think godliness is a means to financial gain.

> People who are afraid to take their car out of the garage should not have purchased the car.

Remember Haggai 2:8: God owns everything. The rich man described in Mark Chapter 10, took ownership of his possessions even though God owns it all. Essentially, it does not matter if we manage little or a lot for God; if we take possession of it, we are not servants of God. We would simply be servants of "stuff". If we claim ownership of the little we have, we are not servants of God. Rather, we are taking possession of stuff that is not ours to claim.

What do I mean by taking possession? I mean, if we think we control and own what we have, we have taken possession of it. If we possess nothing in this world, we certainly are not rich in worldly stuff. The rich man described in Mark Chapter ten, loved stuff. He chose stuff over God. He wanted to spend his wealth on his own pleasures. He trusted stuff more than he trusted God. As I've said before, we cannot serve both money and God. That does not mean we should not enjoy and be thankful for the blessings God bestows on us. We should be content with much just as we should be content with little. If someone puts money and stuff before God, I think it's harder for that person to inherit the Kingdom of God than it is for a real camel to go through the eye of a real needle. Who owns our stuff? If we relinquish our stuff to God by realizing He owns it, we will have treasures in heaven. My wife and I have committed everything to God. Our home is now the servant's quarters and we have to ask permission for everything or be told what to do.

MONEY INFLUENCE

How do we know if money is influencing us? Does money influence us sometimes or all the time? If it does, it is sometimes or always an idol in our lives. I want to discuss some of the ways I evaluate this. Does what we have please God first and us second, or does it only please us? If it only pleases us, we should probably ask God if He wants us to have it. Do we use our money and things for God? Do we use our money and things to increase the resources we have under management for God's glory and purpose? The answer to the last two questions should be yes and if they are yes, it is an indication that we are being good stewards of what God has put under our management and that we are not influenced by money in an unhealthy way.

If we feel like God is leading us to give money as an offering, we should be willing to do this. This is an indication that God is first in our lives. If someone never feels like God is leading them to give money for His purpose or to help others than money is an idol.

> People who are greedy for money have made it an idol in their lives.

Before I purchase something, I like to evaluate whether or not God wants me to make the purchase. I ask myself if God wants me to make the purchase, or is it me who wants to make the purchase. I try to evaluate if I am being selfish. I try to think of how the purchase will benefit God and how it makes

Him look. If money affects our insecurity or contributes to our pride, it's influencing us and has become an idol in our lives.

FEAR

When we have fears over money, it is an idol in our lives. More specifically, fears of not having enough or fears of losing money, makes it an idol in our lives. God promises He will take care of us. Therefore, if we worry about money, we are not trusting God.

> *"Therefore I tell you, do not worry about your life, what you will eat or drink; or about your body, what you will wear. Is not life more important than food, and the body more important than clothes? Look at the birds of the air; they do not sow or reap or store away in barns, and yet your heavenly Father feeds them. Are you not much more valuable than they? Who of you by worrying can add a single hour to his life?"*
> *(Matthew 6:25-27)*

People who are afraid to take their car out of the garage should not have purchased the car. Put in different terms, anyone who is afraid of getting a scratch on their stuff is not putting their treasure in heaven. We must recognize that all earthly treasures will eventually get scratched. Therefore, anyone who is afraid the car will get scratched should buy one that is already scratched.

> *"Do not store up for yourselves treasures on earth, where moth and rust destroy, and where thieves break*

in and steal. But store up for yourselves treasures in heaven, where moth and rust do not destroy, and where thieves do not break in and steal. For where your treasure is, there your heart will be also" (Matthew 6:19-21).

If our heart is with God, we will put our treasure in heaven. Conversely, when we worry about our stuff, we are storing up treasures for ourselves on earth. This does not mean we should be irresponsible by not taking care of what God gives us. When we take care of what He gives us we are being good stewards of what is His.

One way to show God He is first in our lives is to bring Him the first ten percent of what He puts under our management.

GREED

Anyone who is greedy for money is definitely being influenced by money. Remember 1 Timothy 6:10. "Some people eager for money have wandered from the faith and pierced themselves with many griefs". People who are greedy for money have made it an idol in their lives. Traders and investors often make this statement:: "bears make money, bulls make money, and hogs get slaughtered." Anyone who finds they always want more might want to evaluate why this is.

TITHE

God says he wants at least ten percent of our first fruits. Because of this, I want to make sure I give at least ten percent, which is the whole tithe. If I don't give the whole tithe, I cannot expect God to pour out blessings.

> *"Bring the best of the firstfruits of your soil to the house of the LORD your God" (Exodus 23:19).*

> *"Will a man rob God? Yet you rob me. "But you ask, 'How do we rob you?' "In tithes and offerings. You are under a curse—the whole nation of you—because you are robbing me. Bring the whole tithe into the storehouse, that there may be food in my house. Test me in this," says the LORD Almighty, "and see if I will not throw open the floodgates of heaven and pour out so much blessing that you will not have room enough for it. I will prevent pests from devouring your crops, and the vines in your fields will not cast their fruit," says the LORD Almighty (Malachi 3:8-11).*

This is the only place in the Bible that I know of where God says to test Him. It sounds to me like God is challenging us to pay the full tithe. Tithe means tenth. This seems to me like a sure way to have blessing poured out all over us. In Malachi 3:6, God states the descendants of Jacob have turned away from His decrees by not keeping them. God tells His people to return to Him and He will return to them. God's people are the children of Abraham. His people ask how. God tells them they are under a curse because they are robbing Him by not bringing Him the whole tithe.

Jacob was the son of Isaac and Isaac was the son of Abraham.

"Consider Abraham: "He believed God, and it was credited to him as righteousness." Understand, then, that those who believe are children of Abraham. The Scripture foresaw that God would justify the Gentiles by faith, and announced the gospel in advance to Abraham: "All nations will be blessed through you." So those who have faith are blessed along with Abraham, the man of faith" (Galatians 3:6-9).

> Jesus Himself is saying do not neglect the tithe.

Jesus Christ redeemed us. When we receive the Spirit of God, we become brothers and sisters in Christ.

"He redeemed us in order that the blessing given to Abraham might come to the Gentiles through Christ Jesus, so that by faith we might receive the promise of the Spirit" (Galatians 3:14).

Abraham was justified through faith. He believed God. Because of his love for God, he followed God's instructions.

"What then shall we say that Abraham, our forefather, discovered in this matter? If, in fact, Abraham was justified by works, he had something to boast about—but not before God. What does the Scripture say? "Abraham believed God, and it was credited to him as righteousness."

Now when a man works, his wages are not credited to him as a gift, but as an obligation. However, to the man who does not work, but trusts God who justifies the wicked, his faith is credited as righteousness" (Romans 4:1-5).

> There are two reasons that I believe Christians do not tithe which are fear and greed

If we believe God and love Him, we are justified. Because we have been justified though the sacrifice of Jesus Christ, we should show Him our love by putting Him first in our lives. One way to show God He is first in our lives is to bring Him the first ten percent of what He puts under our management.

> *"Is this blessedness only for the circumcised, or also for the uncircumcised? We have been saying that Abraham's faith was credited to him as righteousness. Under what circumstances was it credited? Was it after he was circumcised, or before? It was not after, but before! And he received the sign of circumcision, a seal of the righteousness that he had by faith while he was still uncircumcised. So then, he is the father of all who believe but have not been circumcised, in order that righteousness might be credited to them. And he is also the father of the circumcised who not only are circumcised but who also walk in the footsteps of the faith that our father Abraham had before he was circumcised"* (Romans 4:9-12).

The previous passages are why I personally believe God wants me to tithe. I put my trust in God, so one way I want to demonstrate it is by tithing. The following passage is why I believe God is talking to me in Malachi chapter three.

> *"It is not as though God's word had failed. For not all who are descended from Israel are Israel. Nor because they are his descendants are they all Abraham's children. On the contrary, "It is through*

Isaac that your offspring will be reckoned." In other words, it is not the natural children who are God's children, but it is the children of the promise who are regarded as Abraham's offspring" (Romans 9:6-8).

I also believe that if I tithe, God will bless my tithe; so I demonstrate my belief by tithing. It surprises me how many people claiming to be Christians find reasons not to tithe. I have talked with some people who believe God has told them to pay their bills before they tithe. God is not telling anyone this. God wants the best of our first fruits.

Some followers of Christ argue that the tithe does not apply to the New Testament church. I will not get into the arguments used for this line of thinking. However; people who believe we are not told to tithe in the New Testament will have a very difficult time spinning the following passage.

"Woe to you, teachers of the law and Pharisees, you hypocrites! You give a tenth of your spices — mint, dill and cummin. But you have neglected the more important matters of the law — justice, mercy and faithfulness. You should have practiced the latter, without neglecting the former" (Matthew 23:23).

Read that last sentence again carefully. Jesus Himself is saying do not neglect the tithe.

For anyone still having trouble accepting the fact that God wants us to tithe, please imagine the following two scenarios and determine which one is more likely:

In the first scenario, God looks down and sees John Doe give a tithe to his local church. Seeing this, God calls John's head angel to the throne-room and smacks him in the head. Displeased with John Doe, God might ask John's angel "who told John to tithe? He gave a tithe to the local church and now the church is going to use it to spread the gospel. On top of that, John won't have enough money to pay his electric bill. I know John loves me but how am I supposed to fix this? I promised I would feed and take care of John, but if I take some of his food money and apply it to the electric bill there will not be any money left for food. You are his angel so do not let this happen again. And another thing, get down there and take all his stuff and give it to someone who does not tithe. Doesn't John know this is the New Testament and we can't afford tithes? We are in tough economic times. Things just are not like they were in the Old Testament. Why don't you go ask John how many people he expects me to feed with a fish?"

Here is the second scenario: God looks down and sees John Doe give a tithe and an additional offering to his local church. Seeing this, God calls John's head angel to the throne-room and gives him a high five. God might say, "I like John's display of faith and cheerful giving. Put an extra measure of resources under his management. Push it down and cause it to overflow. He has been faithful with what I have put under his management... increase it."

There are two reasons that I believe Christians do not tithe which are fear and greed. Some fear if they tithe ten percent they will not have enough. Others do not tithe because they think it will cut into their abundance. Non-tithing believers have made money an idol in their lives and will always have less than tithing believers, even if they do not realize it or see it. The material stuff we manage on earth has no eternal substance.

WHAT TO COUNT

How about "Calculating the Tithe"

I tithe ten percent on the gross of all my paychecks. At the first of the month, I tithe on all the paychecks I know I will receive for that month. This is before taxes and all personal expenses. I own a number of businesses. I tithe on the fruits of my businesses and investments when I harvest the fruits. In other words, I tithe on the increase when I receive it from the business. I do not subtract investment losses from gains. This means if I have a capital loss of $2,000 and a capital gain of

$3,000, I tithe $300 not $100. I tithe on all business income as it is passed on to me. If I err, I want to make sure I err in God's favor.

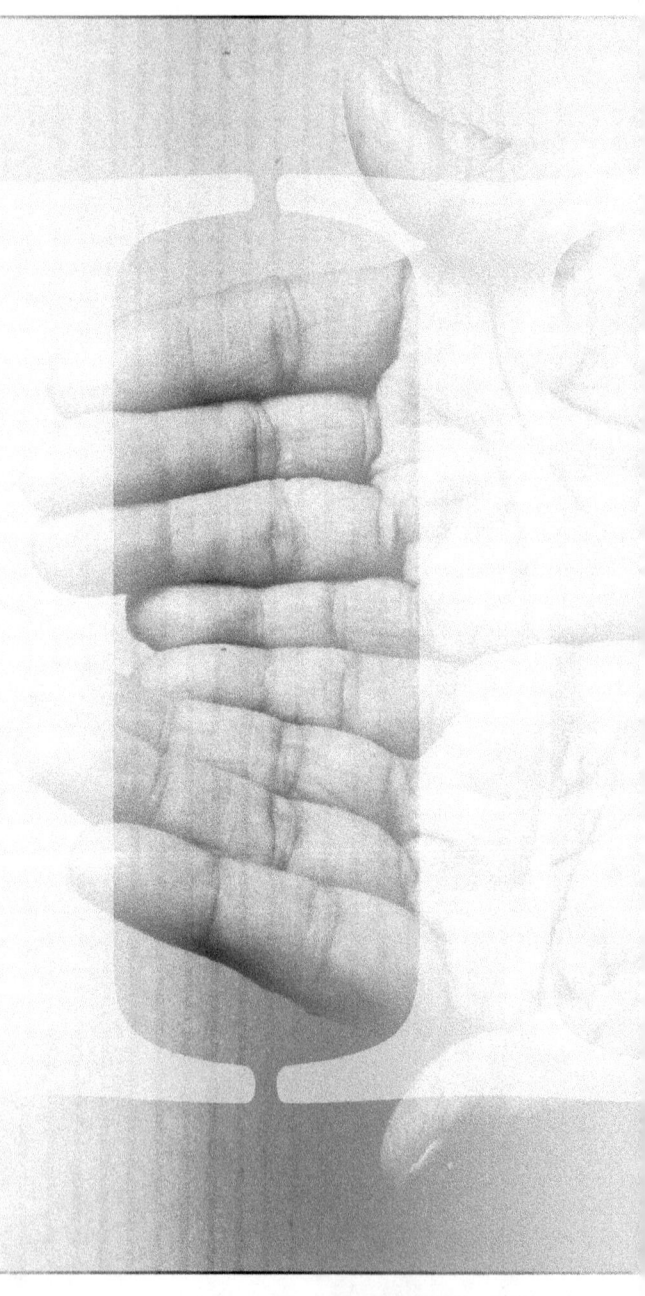

II LETTING GO AND SURRENDER TO GOD

FAITH

"Now faith is being sure of what we hope for and certain of what we do not see. This is what the ancients were commended for" (Hebrews 11:1-2).

I love this verse and this whole chapter. Faith is being certain of what we do not see. Before I had ever been to Mexico, I believed it was there. I trusted what I had heard. When I first traveled to Mexico, it was there. I saw it. If I never acted on my certainty by traveling there, I never would have seen it. If I hear about a great new restaurant, I must drive there in order to taste the food. If I cannot find the restaurant, does that mean it is not there?

Does it matter what we believe? If I believe something enough and with all my heart, will that make it true? I think some people believe that if they believe something enough, that makes it true. Will my beliefs change truth? If I believe something enough, will that change wrong to right? What if I believe rocks are chocolate? What will happen if I bite and chew rocks? Will I taste milky chocolate or will I break my teeth? If I believe rocks are gods, does that make them gods? Can rocks save me?

> If I believe something enough and with all my heart, will that make it true?

> Faith is acting on what we have not yet seen. When I tithe, I see God keep His promise.

Are there multiple ways to God or is there only one way? Can we use a combination of religions or ones that make sense to our little pea brains? Can we make up our own financial rules outside of what God's Word says and be truly blessed by them? Maybe the earth is flat and round. Maybe the earth is a triangle, square, and a hexagon. Columbus did not believe the earth was flat, yet most people in his day disagreed. If any of those people followed Columbus West in their own ship, would they have fallen off the earth because that is what they believed? Any placebo affect would have been irrelevant in this case.

Ultimately, it matters what we believe. God wants us to believe in Him and in His Word, not just in everything we see or everything that seems logical to humans. God's Word is believable, but not everything we hear or think we see is believable. In the day of Columbus, the earth looked flat to most people, but it was not.

> *"And without faith it is impossible to please God, because anyone who comes to him must believe that He exists and that He rewards those who earnestly seek him"* (Hebrews 11:6).

Without faith it is impossible to please God. Faith is acting on what we have not yet seen. When I tithe, I see God keep His promise.

"By faith Noah, when warned about things not yet seen, in holy fear built an ark to save his family. By his faith he condemned the world and became heir of the righteousness that comes by faith" (Hebrews 11:7).

Noah had never seen rain like the rain God said was coming. Noah trusted what God said and acted on it by building an ark. People thought he was a nut, but he still trusted God. If Noah did not believe God and act on what God said to do, he would have drowned. The people who thought what God said was a joke drowned.

If we act on what God says about finances, we trust Him with the finances He has put under our management and we act on our faith. The following are some scriptures we can act on easily.

"Remember this: Whoever sows sparingly will also reap sparingly, and whoever sows generously will also reap generously" (2 Corinthians 9:6).

"Now he who supplies seed to the sower and bread for food will also supply and increase your store of seed and will enlarge the harvest of your righteousness. You will be made rich in every way so that you can be generous on every occasion, and through us your generosity will result in thanksgiving to God" (2 Corinthians 9:10-11).

"Bring the whole tithe into the storehouse, that there may be food in my house. Test

> *me in this," says the LORD Almighty, "and see if I will not throw open the floodgates of heaven and pour out so much blessing that you will not have room enough for it"*
> *(Malachi 3:10).*

> *"Give, and it will be given to you. A good measure, pressed down, shaken together and running over, will be poured into your lap. For with the measure you use, it will be measured to you"*
> *(Luke 6:38).*

I believe that when we act on God's Word, we are demonstrating our certainty of what we do not see.

The point I want to make by displaying the following scripture is not that I think Christians should start testing God by intentionally drinking poison.

> *"And these signs will accompany those who believe: In my name they will drive out demons; they will speak in new tongues; they will pick up snakes with their hands; and when they drink deadly poison, it will not hurt them at all; they will place their hands on sick people, and they will get well"*
> *(Mark 16:17-18).*

If you read the whole passage in context, Jesus rebuked His disciples for their lack of faith as He often did. I am not saying God does not create miracles. He does. My point is that God will create miracles in every area of our lives when we believe Him and act on our faith. God will create miracles in our financial situation if we act on what His Word says. Things that do not seem possible will be possible.

> God has given us authority over all the power of the enemy.

"You foolish man, do you want evidence that faith without deeds is useless? Was not our ancestor Abraham considered righteous for what he did when he offered his son Isaac on the altar? You see that his faith and his actions were working together, and his faith was made complete by what he did." (James 2:20-22).

Remember that our faith and actions must work together in order to make our faith complete.

TRUST GOD

Please do not get distracted over my discussion of faith. It is not my intent to create theological disputes among believers. My goal is to motivate Christians to trust Jesus Christ and Him only. Putting trust in anything on earth is unsafe. Even trusting in what we have seen and known can be dangerous. I would rather trust what God's Word says even if it does not completely make sense to me or cannot be seen by me. I will stand on God's Word.

In Ephesians 6:16 God says, the enemy of Jesus Christ (Satan) throws flaming arrows at us which we can extinguish with faith. God says no weapon formed against us will prosper.

> *"No weapon forged against you will prevail, and you will refute every tongue that accuses you. This is the heritage of the servants of the Lord, and this is their vindication from me," declares the Lord"*
> *(Isaiah 54:17).*

God has given us authority over all the power of the enemy.

> *"I have given you authority to trample on snakes and scorpions and to overcome all the power of the enemy; nothing will harm you"*
> *(Luke 10:19).*

If Satan's weapons are useless against us, how does he attack us? I believe his only chance is to get us to defeat ourselves.

I recently spoke at a local men's breakfast. A friend of mine was there who I used to play softball with. I asked him if he drove his truck to the breakfast. I followed this question up with more questions. "Does anyone else have a set of keys to your truck? Have you ever played a practical joke on anyone? Are you sure your truck is where you parked it?" His answer was, "I'm not sure". Next I picked up an apple off the table and asked another man if he would take me to lunch every day for the next year if I could show him the apple I picked up was a banana. He wanted nothing to do with my challenge. What did I do to these two men? First I isolated them. Then all I did was simply ask them questions that cause them to doubt what they knew as the truth. What did the serpent do to Eve?

We must stand on the Word and keep ourselves surrounded by our brothers and sisters in Christ.

Check it out. Read Genesis.

Satan uses what we can see, touch, smell, hear, taste, and what we cannot see, touch, smell, hear, and taste against us. Our physical senses can lie to us. There is only one thing that cannot lie to us: The Bible. We must stand on the Word and keep ourselves surrounded by our brothers and sisters in Christ. We must believe and act on the Word of God even if it does not always make sense to our five senses. Our brothers and sisters in Christ will constantly remind us of the truth. They will remind us that an apple is an apple and what God says is what we can count on.

> God's opportunities are all around us every day.

God says He will take care of us, not our retirement plans. God knows what we need and He will provide it. I can promise that because that is His promise. We must put our treasure in heaven and not on the lusts of this present world.

Cast but a glance at riches, and they are gone, for they will surely sprout wings and fly off to the sky like an eagle"
(Proverbs 23:5).

On Monday, March 17, 2008, I witnessed a financial giant crumble like a house of cards overnight. I am talking about Bear Stearns, a multi-billion dollar company the day before. Bear Stearns survived with strength through the "Great Depression". Its wealth was depleted on an ordinary day in 2008. Bear Stearns is broke. Employees

> When we keep our eyes on Jesus and trust Him, we will be safe.

were seen on television walking out with cardboard boxes. I wonder if their 401K plans were in those boxes. The news reported that those who thought they were worth millions are now worth very little. Many of their earthly retirements were demolished. Their jobs are lost as are potentially many of their homes.

In May of 2008, the city of Vallejo, California filed bankruptcy. Guess why? Pension plans! Vallejo is not a business, it's a city. Many other supposed financial giants have collapsed since then.

In the book "A God-Made Millionaire", I made some comments about retirement plans that I assumed would be controversial. Actually I make a lot of comments that are controversial. I said that I do not invest in retirement plans because I think they are unsafe and risky. God will worry about tomorrow. I am not going to put His assets under a rock in the form of something that seems secure so that I can take vacation on earth sometime in the future. Maybe things are not always as they appear. God's opportunities are all around us every day. Today has enough worries of its own. God does not want us to store up wealth on earth for our own pleasures in the future. We should be rich toward God now and in the future.

"And he told them this parable: "The ground of a certain rich man produced a good crop. He thought to himself, 'What shall I do? I have no place to store my crops.'

"Then he said, 'This is what I'll do. I will tear down my barns and build bigger ones, and there I will store all my grain and my goods. And I'll say to myself, "You have plenty of good things laid up for many years. Take life easy; eat, drink and be merry."'

"But God said to him, 'You fool! This very night your life will be demanded from you. Then who will get what you have prepared for yourself?'

"This is how it will be with anyone who stores up things for himself but is not rich toward God" (Luke 12:16-21).

> A person's motive when investing in retirement plans is the biggest factor.

I'm not saying that you shouldn't invest in retirement plans. That's for each person to decide and God directs each person differently. I'm merely saying that I don't invest in these types of products and now you know why. I have seen and heard of the Bear Stearns example many times. A person's motive when investing in retirement plans is the biggest factor. The motive should be to build wealth and use it for God. An individual should have a plan on how a retirement plan will be used for God. If someone's plan is to checkout at a certain age and go on permanent vacation, I do not think that is a Godly plan because the motive is wrong. If the plan is to free up your labor for serving God than that is a good plan. I believe we should continue to perform the purpose God has for us

Our God can overcome any financial storm in our lives.

on earth until the day we go to be with Him. I also think the tasks God has for us changes as we age. As we mature spiritually, we become able to perform new tasks. He is always getting us ready for new ministries.

For people who do invest in retirement plans, it is very important to manage it on a regular basis. The investments in a retirement plan should be examined on a weekly basis. You are managing it for God. It is His so take it seriously. Do not just forget about it. Since it's His, you should be a good steward of it.

It's important not to use the lack of investing in retirement plans as an excuse to neglect saving. Saving is a biblical principle and can be used for God when His opportunities arise. I also don't believe that even though God will take care of us, we should avoid planning for the future. Remember, our plans should be committed to and directed by God. He will order our steps. For seven years Joseph prepared for seven years of famine. He did this because God ordered his steps.

When we keep our eyes on Jesus and trust Him, we will be safe. In the following, Peter was able to walk on water until he looked at the storm around him.

"During the fourth watch of the night Jesus went out to them, walking on the lake. When the

disciples saw him walking on the lake, they were terrified. "It's a ghost," they said, and cried out in fear.

But Jesus immediately said to them:

"Take courage! It is I. Don't be afraid."

"Lord, if it's you," Peter replied, "tell me to come to you on the water."

"Come," he said.

Then Peter got down out of the boat, walked on the water and came toward Jesus. But when he saw the wind, he was afraid and, beginning to sink, cried out, "Lord, save me!"

Immediately Jesus reached out his hand and caught him. "You of little faith," he said, "why did you doubt?"

And when they climbed into the boat, the wind died down. Then those who were in the boat worshiped him, saying, "Truly you are the Son of God" (Matthew 14:25-33).

God has promised He will never leave us or forsake us. We do not have to worry about money.

"Keep your lives free from the love of money and be content with what you have, because God has said, 'Never will I leave you; never will I forsake you'" (Hebrews 13:5).

Our God can overcome any financial storm in our lives. He is always right there on the boat with us through any type of trouble.

"Then he got into the boat and his disciples followed him. Without warning, a furious storm came up on the lake, so that the waves swept over the boat. But Jesus was sleeping. The disciples went and woke him, saying, "Lord, save us! We're going to drown!"

He replied, "You of little faith, why are you so afraid?" Then he got up and rebuked the winds and the waves, and it was completely calm.

The men were amazed and asked, "What kind of man is this? Even the winds and the waves obey him!"
(Matthew 8:23-27)

THANKFULNESS

Before we get into the content point, it is a good time to review all the things we are thankful for and thank God for those blessings. Naming and thanking God for all that we have is a good exercise before setting the content point. If you can see, are you thankful for that? If you cannot see, can you hear? If you cannot hear, can you walk? If you cannot walk are you kept warm on cold nights? We can all find many things to be thankful for. Being thankful and thanking God every day for what He has given us will remind us to appreciate all that we have. This will give us contentment. Anyone who is constantly thinking of the things they do not have or want will find contentment to be elusive. God's grace is always sufficient for us.

THORN IN THE FLESH

"To keep me from becoming conceited because of these surpassingly great revelations, there was given me a thorn in my flesh, a messenger of Satan, to torment me. Three times I pleaded with the Lord to take it away from me. But he said to me, "My grace is sufficient for you, for my power is made perfect in weakness. Therefore I will boast all the more gladly about my weaknesses, so that Christ's power may rest on me. That is why, for Christ's sake, I delight in weaknesses, in insults, in hardships, in persecutions, in difficulties. For when I am weak, then I am strong."
(2 Corinthians 12:7-10)

Everything God allows is for His Glory. The passage says Paul had a thorn in his flesh. The thorn was a messenger of Satan. I think this was because Paul was a spiritual giant. Because Paul was a spiritual giant, God did not want spiritual pride to set in. People who really believe God can heal them and do not see a manifest healing could be spiritual giants just like Paul.

Who knows for sure how the thorn in Paul's flesh was manifest, but thorns can manifest in many ways.

If you have a thorn in your flesh it could be because God's power is made perfect in weakness. God's power saves people. Instead of complaining about our troubles that God has not immediately removed, it might be better to thank Him for all the blessings He has given us.

Paul was a person who learned to be content. I believe the following passages are good to ponder before we think about setting our content point.

" Five times I received from the Jews the forty lashes minus one. Three times I was beaten with rods, once I was stoned, three times I was shipwrecked, I spent a night and a day in the open sea, I have been constantly on the move. I have been in danger from rivers, in danger from bandits, in danger from my own countrymen, in danger from Gentiles; in danger in the city, in danger in the country, in danger at sea; and in danger from false brothers. I have labored and toiled and have often gone without sleep; I have known hunger and thirst and have often gone without food; I have been cold and naked." (2 Corinthians 11:24-28)

"For our light and momentary troubles are achieving for us an eternal glory that far outweighs them all." (2 Corinthians 4:17)

The phrase "light and momentary trouble" caught my attention.

III MANAGING AND GROWING RESOURCES

CONTENT POINT

What I call the "content point" is something personal between God and the person developing it. It is a set of rules and guidelines we set for ourselves so that money will not influence us.

"But godliness with contentment is great gain" (1 Timothy 6:6). Wow, godliness with contentment is great gain. That is real! We now have the secret to great gain. Many people are looking for this secret of success on late night real estate infomercials.

Paul is discussing the love of money and contentment in 1 Timothy chapter 6. Godliness with contentment is great gain. Paul makes a point that godliness is not a means to financial gain. We need to check our motive when following God's financial principals. If our motive in following God's principles is to increase wealth and spend it on our pleasures, we have the wrong motive. The resources God puts under our management should be used for what pleases Him. Paul also says "but if we have food and clothing, we will be content with that" (1 Timothy 6:8). That does not mean God does not want to bless us or that He only wants us to have food and clothing. I

> He wants us to be content with whatever we have.

believe He does want to bless us in every way. God has plans to prosper us. I just want to remember that I am the servant and He is my God.

> *"For I know the plans I have for you," declares the LORD, "plans to prosper you and not to harm you, plans to give you hope and a future"*
> *(Jeremiah 29:11).*

In Philippians chapter 4, Paul is thanking the Philippians for their gift and giving glory to God.

> *I rejoice greatly in the Lord that at last you have renewed your concern for me. Indeed, you have been concerned, but you had no opportunity to show it. I am not saying this because I am in need, for I have learned to be content whatever the circumstances. I know what it is to be in need, and I know what it is to have plenty. I have learned the secret of being content in any and every situation, whether well fed or hungry, whether living in plenty or in want. I can do everything through him who gives me strength.*

> *Yet it was good of you to share in my troubles. Moreover, as you Philippians know, in the early days of your acquaintance with the gospel, when I set out from Macedonia, not one church shared with me in the matter of giving and receiving, except you only; for even when I was in Thessalonica, you sent me aid again and again when I was in need. Not that I am looking for a gift, but I am looking for what may be credited to your account. I have received full payment and even more; I am amply supplied, now that I have received from Epaphroditus the gifts you sent. They are a fragrant*

offering, an acceptable sacrifice, pleasing to God. And my God will meet all your needs according to his glorious riches in Christ Jesus.

To our God and Father be glory forever and ever. Amen (Philippians 4:10-20).

God does not want us to have only food and clothes. He wants us to be content with whatever we have. If we only have food and clothing, we should be thankful. This means we should not be greedy for more. If we have a little or a lot, we should be content and thankful for what we have. If God has put millions of dollars under our management, we should be content with that and thankful for the ways He will use it.

Most believers read the Bible but many do not walk, live, and act like the Word of God is true. Those who talk like the Word of God is true and show it in their actions will see miraculous results. How come many of us do not ask God to do supernatural things that line up with His word? I am saying do not put God in a box. If God says something, act on it because it is a fact. God can do miracles in our financial circumstances. We just do not always understand the facts. Godliness with contentment is great gain, period! Let's start with believing "godliness with contentment is great gain". God can make this happen outside of our human logic.

Why does contentment elude us? I am sure

> Those who talk like the Word of God is true and show it in their actions will see miraculous results.

> He wants to provide for us just like we want to provide for our children

we have all thought at one time or another, if I could only make another $500 or $1,000 a month, I would be perfectly happy. The problem is once we have that additional income, we think the same thing all over again.

Imagine the freedom of having no fear of loss and never wanting more. Can we get to a point of complete financial freedom where fear and greed do not influence us? I believe we can. The content point will deliver this with a simple but serious commitment.

I must make a distinction between contentment and the term "content point" which I am using. Contentment has nothing to do with income or the stuff we have. It has nothing to do with our home, car, job, or our current situation. Contentment has to do with being thankful and full of joy in whatever situation we are in. Contentment is being completely satisfied with who we are in Christ and not personally wanting more or feeling guilty about what we have. The "content point" is the personal income we believe God wants us to have in order to serve Him. This can be looked at as the paycheck God wants to pay us for managing the resources He has put under our management. There are some good reasons why God might want our person's paycheck to go up or down. If a couple believes God wants them to have more children, the paycheck might need to go up in order to care for the family the way God wants. God is not cheap. He wants to provide for us just like we want to provide for our children. This family might live in a small apartment. God might want this family to have a home of a certain size in order to better serve Him. A home can be used in wonderful ways for God. My wife and I are so thankful for the ways God uses our home. The ways God uses our home to bless others also blesses us. God might want our personal income to go up for His glory. In the same manner God might want the person paycheck He gives us to go down because of wasteful spending that could be used in wiser ways for Him.

> I believe we can eliminate the influence of money on our lives

What I believe the content point will do by working with the budget formula is help us avoid the temptations of greed and eliminate the fears that can creep into our lives over money.

First we must stop the content point from moving. The problem with the content point is it is a moving target. Once we stop the content point from moving, we can easily hit it. Everyone will have a different content point. The key is to reach it wherever it is. Once we establish the content point, I believe God will begin to work miracles. Within the content point, we will receive an increase even though the content point is not moving higher. This might seem impossible to some, but as I explain it in the budget formula you will see it is NOT impossible.

The first step in setting the content point is through prayer and realizing that God has a personal relationship with each of us. Pray with your family and let God show you where to set the content point. The content point could be a monthly dollar amount that you believe will please God. Even if you lower it below what you are making per month now, you will receive an increase. Only you and God can determine where the content point should be for you. You might raise it thousands of dollars above your current monthly income or you might keep it where it is now. You might even lower it. The important thing is to lock it in. Spend as much time as you need in prayer to determine the content point.

I must emphasize that the purpose of what I call the content point is an attempt to eliminate the influence of money on our lives. Try to be influenced by God more than my example of the content point that will follow. Each person must seek God in determining how to develop the guidelines for the content point. By developing and writing down the guidelines for future income, I believe we can eliminate the influence of money on our lives. Some people might not set a monthly dollar amount as a base for their content point. They might work off of percentages or some other method. That should be directed by God. The goal of the content point is to determine what God wants done with the increase as He brings it. It is easy to rationalize buying a yacht when your income is a million dollars a month. I am not saying do not buy a yacht, but does anyone really need a yacht? God might want a believer to own a yacht. If so, buy one. If the guidelines for the prosperity God plans for us are set before hand and we follow them, money will not influence us.

> A believer's budget should manage the resources God has given in order to fulfill the "Great Commission"

Here are some examples. If your monthly income is $8,000 per month, you might set your content point at $10,000 per month. If you earn $20,000 per month you might set it at $18,000 per month. If you earn $4,000 per month, you might set your content point at $8,000 per month. The content point will have a yearly cost of living increase. If you set your content point at $10,000 per month, it will increase 3% each year for inflation. The second year your content point will be $10,300 per month. Now you have a stationary content point in terms of today's dollars. You will have the same buying power each year.

Now that you have your content point in a dollar amount, it is time to make the simple but serious commitment. Draw up a contract. Put the content point on the contract. Here are the basic rules using a content point of $10,000 per month. You can add as many of your own rules as you would like. $10,000 is what you can spend personally each month. That means when you are earning $1 million per month, you can only spend $10,000 per month personally. That is your content point. Stick to it! You certainly do not need more.

- Content point $10,000

- All income above the content point is used for God's work

> I believe there is so much written in God's word about money because money equals time spent laboring

- 50% of all income above $10,000 goes directly to God's work

- 50% of all income above $10,000 is invested in order to increase God's revenue

- You will get completely out of debt one time and that means everything

- Once debt is completely paid off, new debt must be paid out of the $10,000

Here is another example of a rule my wife and I have. We will only own one home to live in. In other words, we will not own a vacation home. If we want to vacation in a certain place, we will rent. This does not mean we will not own rental properties as an investment for God.

Now you and your spouse sign the contract. If you do not have a spouse, have a witness sign. If you get a spouse, have that person sign it. This will help with accountability.

As we move on to the budget formula, you will see how this works and how you will receive an increase by managing your three budgets that will be created. I must also note that this is not a deal with God. It is just a commitment to serve God with the resources He has put under our management. My Wife's and my content point is a commitment to each other to serve God not our selves.

THE BUDGET FORMULA

A believer's budget should manage the resources God has given in order to fulfill the "Great Commission". Once a person enters into a relationship with Christ, he or she has committed their life to Christ in return for salvation and a more abundant life.

"The thief comes only to steal and kill and destroy; I have come that they may have life, and have it to the full" (*John 10:10*).

Our resources should be committed to Christ. If our whole life is committed to our Lord, then all of our resources will be committed to Him. Our resources include our time, labor, and labor stored in the form of money or other assets.

My wife and I are God's servants. We have realized that the home we live in is the servant's quarters. God decides where the servant's quarters is and what it is. As servants we must be told what to do or ask permission for anything we want to do.

We manage and budget more than just money. We also manage our time and assets. We manage assets such as automobiles and homes. We either manage them well or poorly. The better we manage all resources, the better stewards we will be. We manage our days, weeks, months and years.

> I like going after the card with the lowest balance

I believe God wants time spent with Him every day communicating with Him and studying His word. I also believe one day out of the week should be spent resting and completely committed to God. Time spent every day with God and one day of rest is for our own good. God knows our needs better than we do.

A well diversified budget will also include time spent laboring for God on a weekly or monthly basis. This might include volunteering at your local church or teaching a bible study.

I believe there is so much written in God's word about money because money equals time spent laboring. How we spend it determines where our heart is.

The example of a financial budget I will use is with a $10,000 monthly content point. We will assume $8,000 per month is the current income. Since the income is under the content point, we must start with developing just one budget with an income of $8,000 per month. We will also assume this income is the total household income of a married couple with two children. This is for tax purposes. We will estimate that this family takes home $6,500 after taxes each month including social security.

God says He wants a 10% return on our first fruits. That means He needs a 10% return before anything else happens. $800 goes to the church we attend. That is right;

I believe we should tithe on our gross income. That leaves $5,700 per month. We will estimate the home mortgage at $1,800 per month including all taxes. Monthly bills, such as electricity, cable, telephone, gasoline etc… will be at $900. Automobile expense will be $900 per month which includes two car payments. Food, clothing and insurance will be $1,600 per month. This leaves $500 per month. If there is credit card debt, ouch, we will allot $300 per month for that. This will cover $10,000 in credit card debt. The remaining $200 will be split $100 for investment and $100 for savings. Any excess from the budget should be added to savings every month. Be disciplined. Don't spend the excess or carry it over to the next month.

> Keep the card with the lowest interest rate

TITHE	$800
Taxes	$1,500
Mortgage	$1,800
Bills	$900
Auto	$900
Food & Clothing/Insurance	$1,600
Credit Card	$300
Investment	$100
Savings	$100
Total	$8,000

GETTING OUT OF DEBT

First we will focus on the debt. From the example above, let's say we have three credit cards. One credit card has a balance of $5,000 and carries an annual interest rate of 15%. The next credit card has a balance of $4,000 and carries an annual interest rate of 12%. The last credit card has a balance of $1,000 and carries an interest rate of 13%. In addition to the credit cards, let's say the balance on the mortgage is $250,000 and it carries a very low 6% annual percentage rate on a 30 year fixed mortgage. We will include two car payments. The first is $350 per month and has three years left on a five year term. The second payment is $400 per month and only has one year of payments remaining.

There are two strategies I like for getting out of credit card debt. The first is focusing on the credit card with the highest interest rate. The second is focusing on the card with the lowest balance. I like going after the card with the lowest balance more than the card with the highest interest rate. The card with the lowest balance is $1,000. The minimum payment on this card would be about $20 per month. The minimum payment on the card with a balance of $5,000 would be about $75 per month. The minimum payment on the card with the $4,000 balance would be about $50 per month. We have allotted $300 per month for credit card debt. We must pay $75 on one and $50 on the next. This leaves $175 that can be paid on the card with the lowest balance.

In about six months the first card will be paid off. Next, begin paying $225 on the second card with the $4,000 balance. In another six months this card will be paid down to a balance of about $2,800.

This completes the first year. $1,200 has been saved and $1,200 has been put into a brokerage account. One credit card has been completely paid off and the automobile with the $400 payment has also been paid off. This frees up another $400 per month.

The next step is to add $100 per month to the investment account and $300 to the credit card being paid off. $525 per month is being paid toward the card that started with the $4,000 balance. In about six months this card will be paid off.

Tithe	*$800*
Taxes	*$1,500*
Mortgage	*$1,800*
Bills	*$900*
Auto	*$500*
Food & Clothing/Insurance	*$1,600*
Credit Card	*$600*
Investment	*$200*
Savings	*$100*
Total	*$8,000*

Now begin paying $600 per month on the last credit card. In about eight months this card will be paid off. You will now be two months into the third year. There is now only ten months left on the second car payment. You have over $2,600 in savings and over $4,500 in your brokerage account that has been invested. I will discuss the investments later. Now is a good time to add a $50 monthly offering above your tithe.

After twenty-six months, there is no credit card debt and one automobile has been paid off. You have freed up $550 to continue paying debt. You added to the investment account and the offering. Each time you pay off a credit card cut it up but do not cancel the account. This will help to keep your credit score stronger. Sometimes canceling accounts lowers your credit score. Keep the card with the lowest interest rate and try to increase the credit card line of credit for emergencies.

Tithe	*$800*
Offering	*$50*
Taxes	*$1,500*
Mortgage	*$1,800*
Bills	*$900*
Auto	*$1,050*
Food & Clothing/Insurance	*$1,600*
Investment	*$200*
Savings	*$100*
Total	*$8,000*

$50 has been added to God's work every month. You have freed up $550 per month. Now apply the $550 per month to the last car payment. It will be paid off in four months. In two and a half years you have paid off your automobile debt and all credit card debt. Notice, you and God have received an increase. You are not even at the content point of $10,000 per month yet. Let's adjust the budget at this point.

It has been two and a half years. Let's say you have received a pay raise of $200 per month. You are now earning $8,200 per month. The tithe is $820 per month. Let's add another $80 per month as an offering. You have about $5,300 in your investment account and over $3,000 in savings. After the tithe and offering, you should still have about the same $5,700 per month. However, you have increased the amount of money paid toward God's Kingdom and you are out of debt except for your mortgage payment.

The mortgage payment is still $1,800 per month. Bills are now $1,000. Food, clothing and insurance are $1,850. This leaves $550 for investing and $550 for savings. We have increased the savings at this time because the cars may only have a couple years left. At the end of the third year, you have about $9,000 in your investment account and over $6,300 in savings.

Tithe	*$820*
Offering	*$130*
Taxes	*$1,500*
Mortgage	*$1,800*
Bills	*$1,000*
Food & Clothing/Insurance	*$1,850*
Investments	*$550*
Savings	*$550*
Total	*$8,200*

> The bottom line is God can do whatever He wants

From the beginning of this adventure you should be praying in a manner described in the chapter on prayer. This will give you the wisdom needed and allow God to order your steps in building wealth for Him.

Now that you have demonstrated good stewardship, believe God will do what He says He will do. Let's say you feel like God has been putting on your heart a new business venture so you start a small business. You can do it. Starting a business is easy. Every business we have ever heard of was started by someone so why not you? Follow the passion and wisdom God has given you.

Let's say you do not want to quit your job yet, but you borrow $75,000 and start that business. You hire a couple part time employees and work part time yourself.

God has blessed your business. At the end of the first year in business, it is profiting $3,000 per month after taxes and all business expenses. It is getting fun now.

At the end of the fourth year since your commitment, you have about $16,000 in your investment account and about $13,000 in saving. You have an additional $3,000 in monthly income because of the business you started. Your gross income is actually $1,000 over your content point, but you still have not hit your content point. You will see as we go. At this point you would add $300 per month to the tithe and you could add $200 to the offering. This leaves $2,500 in additional income per month so add $1,000 to the saving and $1,000 to the brokerage account each month. God is blessing you. Also add $500 to your personal budget each month. You are now adding $1,500 to the investment account and $1,550 to savings every month.

At the end of the fifth year, you have about $36,000 in your investment account and $32,000 in savings. In addition to this, your business is doing well. It is now generating $10,000 in cash monthly after taxes and expenses. Let's say you also have about $50,000 in a business savings account because you have only been taking $3,000 per month out of your business.

Now you can take about $45,000 out of your business savings. Pay $4,500 for the tithe and $1,000 for an offering. God is blessing you. Trade in your cars and buy two new ones. We will estimate the trade in value for the cars is an average of $10,000 each. You just bought two $30,000 vehicles and still do not have a car payment. I think you are getting the idea from this example so let's jump to the tenth year.

You have quit your job and are working in your business full time. It is bringing a profit of $25,000 per month. You now have

> "Past performance is no indication of future performance"

$150,000 in your investment account. You have purchased two investment properties with the money you have been putting in savings. You still have $30,000 in savings and have added two duplexes so you have four tenants.

Now we need to go back to the content point because it is definitely in play at this point. God has blessed you and you have stayed committed to your content point. You have not spent more than $10,000 per month personally in the last ten years. You have added to the tithe, offering, investments, and savings. If we adjust the $10,000 monthly income to equal the same value it was ten years ago it would be $13,439. This is a 3% cost of living increase for each of the ten years. Your content point has not gone up. Because of inflation, $13,439 buys what $10,000 bought ten years ago.

An option at this point is to sell one of the duplexes and your house in order to pay cash for a new home. Pay the tithe on the profit from the sales. You are now completely out of debt and have $25,000 per month coming in after business taxes and expenses. Your business is running smoothly and requires very little of your time. You now have three budgets that need to be managed.

The first budget is your personal budget which is also your content point. Let's say you set it at $13,000 per month which is actually under your content point by $439.

All income above this dollar amount pays for taxes, investments, and God's work.

Here is an example for your $13,000 monthly budget. Remember things will probably cost more ten years from the time you started this commitment. $2,500 per month goes toward bills such as electricity, housekeeping, yard maintenance, cable, and garbage. $1,000 per month will be used for auto insurance and gasoline, although you might not be buying gas. $3,000 per month will be allotted for food and clothing. Let's create a budget line for entertainment at $3,500 per month. This would include eating out, movies, and weekend getaways. This leaves $3,000 per month. Put it in savings for future expenses such as automobiles and vacations. The business covers health insurance in addition to all taxes.

Now we will address the second budget. This budget is $6,000 per month and is used for personal taxes, investments and increasing God's assets. This is 50% of what you earn above your content point. This is $72,000 per year and can be used for starting or buying businesses, real estate, or investing through your brokerage account.

The third budget is used for God's work. This is also $6,000 per month and well above a 10% tithe. I would put $3,000 toward your local church and the other $3,000 toward an offering of God's leading

> When I buy stock, I am buying a piece of a business

During an economic downturn, some businesses contract and the price of their stock goes down

each month. This is the fun part of the budget because it is what you use for feeding and clothing those in need. This can also be used for missionaries, which is valuable labor. The labor missionaries spend might be the most valuable labor. Yes, it is more valuable than the most expensive athletes' labor.

The second and third budgets will increase significantly every year. In general, 50% of all income above the content point and after business expenses and taxes goes to the second budget. 50% goes to the third budget.

The $72,000 per year in the second budget can grow very rapidly. For those of you who read "A God Made Millionaire" you know the $72,000 can be leveraged in order to buy an existing business with very good cash flow. It is possible to double the money in three years or less when wise business choices are made.

The bottom line is God can do whatever He wants. If someone has the right heart and follows biblical principles, miracles will happen.

Let's recap the basics of this budget formula. Always tithe ten percent on total income received and give offerings as God leads. Excess above the content point pays for taxes and the tithe as long as the whole tithe on total income is paid. If the content point is $10,000 per month and the total income is $12,000 per month, the $2,000 excess pays the $1,200 tithe plus offerings. The additional excess is applied toward taxes. If total income is $20,000 on the same content point, there is an excess of $10,000. The $2,000 tithe and a $3,000 offering is paid from this excess. There is still a $5,000 excess. Taxes are taken out of this remaining amount. What is remaining of the excess is re-invested in order to make God's income increase.

Investors are influenced by fear and greed

Here is how it looks. The first budget is the personal budget equal to the content point of $10,000. Fifty percent of the income above $10,000 goes directly to God. This is $5,000. The other fifty percent above the content point is applied to taxes and re-investing. If taxes are $3,000 per month, then the last $2,000 is re-invested.

Here is a basic diagram that will help to understand the three budgets with $30,000 in monthly income and a content point of $10,000.

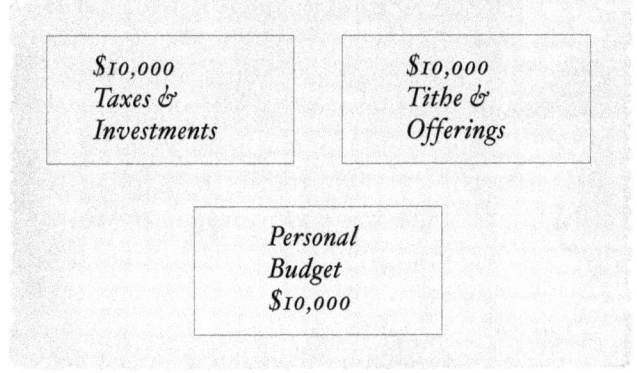

INVESTING

Buy low and sell high, right? This sounds so simple but why is it so hard. Why do so many people buy high and sell low?

Money supply affects supply and demand

In every company prospectus, you will find this phrase "past performance is no indication of future performance". Investors should take this to heart more than most do. This comment is overlooked or swept to the side so often. Many financial advisors say "in the long run the market always goes up". Maybe it always has but why does that mean it always will. Maybe the market will go up in the future or maybe it will go down. I predict it will either go up OR down in the near future and in the long run.

In order to become a great investor, an individual must understand what money is and the value of labor. People who have read "A God Made Millionaire" know I view money as labor. Money is one place we park our labor. A person who earns $300 in ten hours earns $30 per hour. Once payment is received, ten hours of labor has been converted into money. If that $300 is used to buy a household appliance, labor has now been transferred to the appliance. Ten hours of labor is now stored in the form of a household appliance. The appliance has a value of ten hours of labor. If the appliance is sold for $150 to someone who earns $150 per hour, labor has now been

96

transferred back into the form of money. However; five hours of labor just vanished. In this case, the original person who bought the appliance bought high and sold low.

Let's look at this example a different way. John earns $30 per hour. Mike earns $150 per hour. Ted earns $10 per hour. John bought the appliance for ten hours of his labor. He sold it to Mike for one hour of Mike's labor which is five hours of John's labor. When John's labor was converted back into money, it had been devalued. John's ten hours of labor is now worth $150 in the form of money.

One hour of Mike's labor has been transferred to the appliance. If Mike sells the appliance to Ted for $200, he just transferred his one hour of labor back into the form of money but now his one hour of labor is worth $200 per hour. Ted spent twenty hours of his labor for the appliance.

When I buy stock, I am buying a piece of a business. I transfer money into the form of business assets. Business assets have many forms. Office furniture, inventory, cash, labor, branding, management, and technology are some of the forms. If I am able to transfer the business assets in the form of stock, back into money at a higher value, I just bought low and sold high. Every time a stock is purchased, either the buyer or seller made a good choice. The other made a bad choice.

> People will pay more than the true value of the home when interest rates are low

I especially like it when the CEO (the top executive) buys large amounts of stock in his company consistently

Stock values go up and down due to the value of the underlying business and supply and demand for the stock. The value of a business is determined by its ability or potential to earn income and turn that income into increasing profits. Supply and demand is determined by the number of stock shares available for purchase and the number of buyers willing to purchase stock.

Labor in the form of money is used to purchase assets. People who are good at this multiply their labor just like Mike did in the previous example.

It is difficult to determine the value of a business. There are a lot of variables such as trends, macro-economic cycles, product cycles, and earnings growth. Remember, when someone buys stock, they are buying a business.

A long term trend could lay the foundation for a new business or product. A new business in a new trend has the potential to grow earning quickly and for an extended period of time providing the management is sound. For instance, increasing gasoline prices could generate a need and want for electric automobiles. New electric cars would demand the creation of new industries. There would be a need for service stations that could charge electric cars and new technology to service electric cars. These developments would eventually drive down the earnings of oil companies and the price of their stock.

Incidentally, on the subject of the environment and climate change while I do not believe climate change, either cooling or warming, can be caused by man, this is not an excuse to pollute or waste resources. Neither is it an excuse to waste energy. Wasting energy is no different than wasting God's resources. Just because I believe eating meat is okay, doesn't mean I should eat ten pounds of it every day. Polluting damages that which God has given us. Christians are called to be good stewards of what He has given us. That includes the earth we live on.

> It is important to know when debt can be converted back to money

Macro-economic cycles have to do with the overall economies of a country and of the world. The economy goes through phases. It goes up and it goes down. During an economic downturn, some businesses contract and the price of their stock goes down. Other stocks can benefit from an economic downturn. Money flows into stocks of businesses that provide necessities such as food, pharmaceuticals and toothpaste. These are called non-cyclical stocks and have a tendency to maintain consistent earnings. Cyclical stocks such as the stock of automobile companies appreciate when economic times are good. Another example of a cyclical stock is the stock of a company that benefits from the Christmas season.

Product cycles are influenced by the life of a product. An example of this is video tapes. Video tapes have been replaced by

> If leverage is misused, it can be worse than bad debt

DVDs. Another example of this is that digital cameras are replacing cameras that require film. The technology behind a product does not last forever.

Stocks have what is called a P/E ratio. A P/E ratio is price to earnings ratio. This is the current price divided by the yearly earnings. Earnings are the profit. If ABC stock is selling for $9 per share and the company earns $1.50 per share, the P/E ratio is 6. In today's market environment, this would be considered excellent value. This means the underlying business is increasing its assets by $1.50 per share each year. Theoretically the stock value would go up $1.50 per share each year. Anyone who invests regularly and understands the stock market knows this is not what usually happens. ABC stock could double in a year or it could go down to $3 per share even though $9 per share is an excellent value.

Why does this happen? The answer is supply and demand. Investors are influenced by fear and greed. When fear creeps into the market, stocks go down. When greed creeps into the market, stocks go up.

Sometimes a stock is purchased well above its value and sold for even a higher value. This is because the demand is high. In early 2000 people were buying some stocks with P/E ratios well over 100 or stocks that did not even have a P/E ratio. Some of the businesses underlying these stocks were worthless. Some of them had very poor management and had no business being in business. All some of these businesses had was what many investors considered a good idea. A good idea is not a business. We all know what happened. Many of these stocks crashed along with the market.

> Money is labor not green air.

Sometimes a stock is purchased at a great value but goes down. This is because the demand is low compared to the supply. If I were to buy gold at $100 per ounce, everyone knows I got a great value. That does not mean gold cannot go down to $50 per ounce. If no one wants gold, the price will go down.

There are many variables that influence supply and demand. If ABC has excellent management with a proven track record of managing the business assets well, the management will use the $1.50 in earnings per share to increase earnings and grow the business. In this case the demand for ABC stock would be high and could drive the P/E ratio up to 12 or higher. This would double the stock price. If a business makes more money every year, eventually its stock will go up. If investors think the business will lose money in the future, its stock will go down.

Economic cycles are influenced by money supply. Money supply is influenced by interest rates. The more we understand

> Many people have lost their future labor in the form of debt...

the supply of money, the bigger advantage we will have when investing. Remember, money represents labor. It is used in a modern day bartering system. Our labor is used to produce products that can be sold.

Money supply affects supply and demand. Interest rates affect the cost of labor. An easy way to see how this all ties together is to use an example of purchasing a home. Property tax and other fees are excluded in this example. In order to simplify this example we will also say there is no down payment on the home. If I purchase a home for $200,000 and the interest rate on a thirty-year mortgage is 9%, my payment will be about $1,610 per month. I will pay $579,330 over thirty years for the home. If interest rates go down to 5.5%, I could buy this same home for about $1,135 per month for thirty years. I would pay $408,808 over thirty years for this same home purchased for $200,000. The reason for this is because I was able to borrow labor at a lower price. It now takes less of my labor to pay off the home over thirty years and less of my labor to make the monthly payments.

Lower interest rates will make a $200,000 home more affordable for more people. This will increase the demand for the home. The increased demand will cause the price of the home to go up. More people will buy homes and shrink the supply until homes are overvalued. People will pay more than the true value of the home when interest rates are low. This causes inflation. The Federal Reserve Bank will increase interest rates in order to stifle inflation and the cycle repeats itself.

Understanding economic conditions and cycles are a big benefit when investing. The objective is to buy low and sell high or at least to sell higher than the purchase price.

Interest rates affect stock prices. When interest rates are low, more businesses and stocks are purchased. This drives stock prices up. The demand for stocks also goes up because low interest rates provide low yields in money markets and fixed income investment products. Low yields motivate investors to move money into products that provide the potential of a higher return.

Management is a very important component of a successful business. Businesses that are managed poorly are doomed. It is not wise to buy the stock of an underlying company with bad management. When investing, it is important to do your homework on the management team. Research and evaluate the experience and track record of the management team. When we buy stock, we are investing in the management team not just a product or service.

> When over leveraged assets depreciate, the "smoke and mirror" financial structure crashes and burns

> Sooner or later, someone is going to get caught with their hand in the cookie jar

One of my favorite and most effective ways to evaluate a company and its management is to look at insider trading. Insiders are officers and directors of the company. These are the leaders and decision makers in a business. They hold titles such as Chief Executive Officer (CEO), Chief Financial Officer (CFO), Chief Operating Officer (COO), Director, President, and Chairman of the board. When they are buying up the stock of the company they own and manage this is an indication they are confident in themselves and their company. They would not be buying stock unless they believe it is undervalued and will increase in value sometime in the future. I especially like it when the CEO (the top executive) buys large amounts of stock in his company consistently. The CEO has more knowledge of himself or herself and of the company than anyone. If the CEO is selling stock on a regular basis, this is a huge red flag. If multiple insiders are selling stock this is also a huge red flag. There is no explanation insiders can give me for multiple insiders selling. I am skeptical of everything people say. Sometimes insiders paint a rosy picture of the company while they are selling and give reasons why they are selling. I prefer to look at people's actions. If insiders are buying, I am buying. If they are selling, I am selling.

I also like to evaluate a company's debt-to-equity ratio. I rarely buy stock in companies that have debt-to-equity ratios of greater than 1. The debt-to-equity ratio is calculated by dividing the debt by the equity (debt/equity). Equity is equal to the net worth. If a company has total assets of $10,000,000 and its debt is $5,000,000, there is $5,000,000 in equity. $5 million/$5 million is 1. I consider a debt to equity ratio of less than 1 to be acceptable in most cases. Some debt, as long as it is used for an asset will increase profits in most cases. This is of course, if the management of the company knows what they are doing. Here is what I mean by that. If I go out to dinner and put the meal on a credit card, then eat the meal, I just consumed the asset. I am only left with debt. If I buy a business for $1,000,000 by putting $500,000 down, I have an asset worth $1,000,000 and debt on that asset of $500,000. My debt-to-equity ratio would be 1. I could always convert the asset back to money then pay off the debt. It is important to know when debt can be converted back to money. This is different than purchasing $5,000 in products on a credit card then consuming the products. In this case nothing can be converted back to money in order to pay off the debt because the assets have been consumed.

There are many ways to determine if a company is growing. A company that consistently grows its assets, equity, and profits will consistently increase its stock price in the long run. Growth can be measured by return on assets, return on equity, and projected earnings per share growth.

DEBT

When managing and budgeting resources, it is very important to understand debt. Some debt is bad and some debt is not really debt at all.

Many people hire investment advisors or money managers

Ninety-nine percent of the time, credit card debt is bad. Assets are convertible to money and money is convertible to labor. Most products or services purchased with credit cards are consumable. If debt is carried on a credit card it is unwise. The person who purchases and consumes products purchased with credit cards literally becomes a slave to credit card debt. Let me explain. Let's say I earn $20 per hour. If I spend $1,000 on a credit card eating out, I have consumed the products purchased with the $1,000. I basically ate my future labor. I will have to spend about two and a half hours of my labor every week for the next two years to pay off what I ate. That is sixty hours of my labor. I am paying back the $1,000 plus interest.

Here is a basic rule to follow. If acquired debt is not backed up by an appreciable asset, the debt is usually bad. If I use credit to purchase an automobile, that will depreciate, that debt is probably bad. In some cases automobile debt can be beneficial. However; it takes a sharp pencil and an expert to figure out the variables of the time value of money, inflation, and possible tax benefits. This is not something a financial novice should attempt. The best approach for most people is to pay cash for anything that will not go up in value.

If I use credit to acquire an appreciable asset, I can always convert the asset to cash, pay off the debt and put some money/labor in my pocket. The key here is that the debt and asset are interchangeable. If I sell the asset, I can pay off all the debt and still have money left. If I put dinner on a credit card, I cannot sell the dinner I just bought and pay off the debt. Why, because I ate the dinner.

An understanding of return on assets (ROA) and return on investment (ROI) is beneficial. Here is an example of (ROA). If I purchase a home for $200,000 and five years later that home is worth $250,000, I made $50,000 in five years. The (ROA) over five years is $50,000 / $200,000 = 25%.

(ROI) has a bigger impact in this case. If I put $50,000 down on the same home purchased for $200,000, and the value of the home goes up to $250,000 in five years my (ROI) over a five year period is 100%. I invested $50,000 and earned $50,000 in five years. This is called leveraging. If leverage is misused, it can be worse than bad debt.

The recent credit problems in the United States are a result of bad and excessive leveraging decisions. Greed is the underlying cause. Greed causes people to want a bigger (ROI) so they buy assets by using more credit and less money/labor. Assets can fluctuate. They do not always just go up in value. Sometimes they go down. The stock market goes up and down on its long term journey up. Bear Sterns is an example of a powerhouse company that made bad leveraging/credit decisions.

ECONOMY

When investing or managing resources, I believe it's very important to understand what has caused the economic problems of 2008-2009 and perhaps longer.

Leverage created this. The way I like to explain it is by once again using labor as an example. Remember the discussion about debt? Overleveraging can be a consequence of greed and a lack of patience. Anyone who purchases a business or any other type of asset is doing so in the hopes that the asset will appreciate. That means the value will go up and can be sold for a profit.

Money is labor not green air. When credit is used to purchase an asset, future labor that has not been performed yet is used to purchase that asset. The borrowed money is transferred into the asset. Overleveraging in residential real estate is just one place where the problem began. Banks and mortgage companies who were greedy for greater profit made loans to impatient and materialistic people. Loans were made to people with poor credit; people with a poor track record of accumulating enough labor to pay off the labor they borrowed. The biggest problem was that the homes purchased were fully leveraged. Here is an example that highlights this problem: A home purchased for $250,000 was purchased on one hundred percent credit, or borrowed labor without equity or cushion in the asset. The mortgage debt on a $250,000 home was $250,000 plus interest. When people who purchased homes like this couldn't earn enough money through their labor to pay what was owed each month, the downward spiral began.

Easy money was the culprit. Remember, when interest rates are lowered, the money supply goes up. When the money supply goes up, inflation causes problems. This is because an artificial increase in money is not supported by labor. Just because there are two paper bills available for spending, it does not mean there is more labor earning that paper. If a widget cost one dollar backed by true labor, the widget is worth one dollar's worth of labor. When the money supply goes up, that does not mean the value of the widget goes up. The widget now costs one real dollar backed by labor and one fake dollar.

Many people couldn't earn enough real money in their lifetime to pay for the purchases they made with fake money. Many people have lost their future labor in the form of debt which has enslaved them. Sooner or later the money spent must be backed by an honest day's work for an honest wage.

If someone purchased a $250,000 home by saving $70,000, the mortgage debt would only be $180,000. The mortgage payment would be manageable and there would be an equity cushion in the home. If the home depreciated down to $180,000, the home could still be sold with only a loss of past labor, not future labor.

People and companies have tried to get a return on investment (ROI) with nothing invested. Remember, money is not green air.

The Bear Sterns example and many others are also part of the problem. Investments in businesses, stocks and other assets were over leveraged in the hopes that the asset would appreciate. This is a form of Russian-Roulette. When over leveraged assets depreciate, the "smoke and mirror" financial structure crashes and burns.

Simply stated, financial institutions lost money because of foolish loans made out of greed. These losses cause people to lose their jobs and the problem compounds. People who thought money was green air came to learn that they have no more monopoly money to spend. When monopoly money is exposed for what it really is, even people who have been good stewards can get burned.

The loss of equity and jobs causes even responsible people to lose businesses and even more jobs causing a downward spiral until reality hits. Money is not green air. It must be backed by labor that produces true value. Supply and demand must determine the value of labor, not need, want or unions.

Many companies are forced by unions to pay unfair-high wages that do not follow the laws of supply and demand. Many CEO's are paid huge salaries and astronomical bonuses for poor performance. They are being paid fake money for the green air that was earned in the past. Let's say I am hired by a chair maker to make chairs. If he takes me into a room that has ten chairs in it and tells me to make ten just like it, I should get paid for performance. If I lose five chairs instead of making ten, when the chair maker comes back and sees only five chairs, should he give me a ten-million dollar bonus just because I tell him there are fifteen invisible chairs? I don't think that would be the case. He most likely will demand payment for the five lost chairs instead of considering paying me a bonus.

So what is happening right now in 2009? Presidents are not stupid even though all of us can probably pick at least one out who we think was. None of them are. This probably cannot be said for all politicians, but the real problem is that none of them want to get caught with their hand in the cookie jar. Even the ones that are very smart know sooner or later, someone is going to get caught with their hand in the cookie jar.

The government is printing green air and spending future labor. Our population is not growing quickly enough to offset the labor deficit that is being created. What's worse is that our current employers are using their labor to pay employees who are not producing the labor they are being paid for. So how is this happening? Many companies and employees are being over paid for the labor they are performing. They are getting paid more than the value they are producing. Where is the money coming from? It is coming from laborers who give part of their labor to the government in the form of taxes. Now, the government is taking this money and giving it to people who have not earned it. As a matter of fact, they lost it through unproductive labor.

Oil has plummeted from about $150 a barrel down to $33 a barrel. While it has recently risen up again, it remains well below its peak. This has occurred because of the contraction in the economy. The decline in the value of assets is due to lost jobs and the removal of credit provided by banks.

This prevents people from spending fake money which artificially inflates the economy. When people have less money to spend on gasoline, the price of a barrel of oil goes down. When oil goes down, oil producing countries have less money to spend on American products and products from other countries.

The government has lowered interest rates as low as possible. Interest rates cannot go below zero. Mortgage rates are the lowest in history. People are beginning to refinance mortgages. Why wouldn't they? Money is free, or at least that is how it appears. The problem, as we all have been painfully reminded of, is that nothing is free.

So what will happen? Probably what has happened in the past is coming. With the money supply increasing at an accelerated rate never seen before, our "microwave" or "compulsively consumable" society will begin spending all the fake money circulating through people's hands. The "smoke and mirror" economy will again be re-established. Inflation will increase and the cycle will start all over again. If oil at $150 a barrel seemed high, what will oil look like when it reaches over $150 a barrel? The United States dollar will crash because it's not supported by an honest day's wage for an honest day's labor. It will take more green air to buy real value.

The expansion of drilling for oil in the United States has been all but forgotten.

People are already beginning to buy gas guzzling trucks and SUVs once again. The economy will behave like a yo-yo; it's near the bottom of the string now and I believe it will rapidly rise to the top of the string in a flame-like fashion. The government will try to slow the rapid rise by raising interest rates in an attempt to cool inflation. The decrease in fake money supply will stop spending in its tracks. I have a feeling the yo-yo will move back down with such speed that it will break the string at the bottom.

So what should we do? I am not a prophet, but my instincts tell me and in turn I am telling you to look to the only sure thing I know, which is to faithfully trust God.

If my sense is correct, great wealth will be made in oil and other commodities. The price of food and gasoline will skyrocket. Oil can be bought through ETFs such as USO and OIL. It can also be bought through oil companies such as Exxon Mobil Corp (XOM), W&T Off Shore Inc (WTI), oil trust like PGH, and HTE.

Be aware that there is a danger in buying stocks or investing in some assets in bad economic times. Individual businesses can go out of business. If this happens a complete loss of the investment will occur. Buying stocks at very low prices that have been decreasing have a good chance of going to zero. However to be clear, I must emphasize that this is only my opinion.

SETTING UP A BROKERAGE ACCOUNT

Many people hire investment advisors or money managers. This can be a wise idea. However; it is very important to understand how the relationship between the investor and the investment advisor works. Conflicts of interest are extremely common and are often difficult to avoid.

I am a business owner, consultant, business coach and "Accredited Asset Management Specialist" (AAMS). I have a friend who is a financial consultant. He is a strong believer in Christ and I have known him since we were both in third grade. We often talk about the difficult conflicts that can arise in the industry.

The situation I advise people to proceed with caution about or, better yet to avoid altogether, is a relationship with an advisor who earns money by selling financial products. In this case, the person selling the product makes money regardless of whether the client does or doesn't. Commissions are received on products sold and the advisors often have monthly quotas to meet. The potential for a conflict of interest is obvious to see here.

When interviewing a potential financial advisor, it's important to make sure the advisor's interests match the clients. In this case, either a win-win or a lose-lose will occur. Many money managers who are not selling products for a commission fall into the first category. If the money manager earns money by maximizing and preserving the client's assets, this is a possible beneficial structure for the advisor and client. Caution is still advised. Even experienced financial advisors can lose a lot of money.

Another option is to set up your own brokerage account and hire an advisor for a fee to consult. Of course any investor can set up his or her own account and begin trading without an advisor. For a beginner or novice investor, this is most likely to become a very expensive education.

A brokerage account is required in order to invest in stocks and other investment products. There are many brokers to choose from. Do not be intimidated by the term broker. Setting up a brokerage account is simple to do online and requires very little capital in most cases.

Here are some choices:

E*Trade
us.etrade.com/e/t/home

Scottrade
www.scottrade.com

TD/Ameritrade
www.tdameritrade.com/welcome1.html

Charles Schwab
www.schwab.com

Trade Station
www.tradestation.com/default_2.shtm

Fidelity
www.fidelity.com

This is certainly not a complete or exhaustive list, so it is important to research all brokerage houses in order to choose the one that's best for you. They all charge different fees and provide different services.

IV ENGAGING AND SERVING GOD

PRAYER

Jesus tells us how to pray by giving us an example. This is called "The Lords Payer".

"This, then, is how you should pray: 'Our Father in heaven, hallowed be your name, your kingdom come, your will be done on earth as it is in heaven. Give us today our daily bread. Forgive us our debts, as we also have forgiven our debtors. And lead us not into temptation, but deliver us from the evil one.' For if you forgive men when they sin against you, your heavenly Father will also forgive you. But if you do not forgive men their sins, your Father will not forgive your sins" (Matthew 6:9-14).

> When we are in heaven, everything will make sense

First He starts off by praising His Father. Then He asks that the Father will have His way on earth, just like He has His way in heaven. There is full knowledge in heaven. When we are in heaven, everything will make sense. We will see that what God wants and that which he has done is perfect. Jesus is asking for what His Father wants, not what He wants.

He asks for daily bread, which is only what He needs today. He is also praying for something God has promised us. He is

> It's not about us. It's about God

not asking for something He wants or even needs a year from now. He asks the Father to forgive our sin because we have forgiven anyone who has sinned against us. If we do not forgive others, the Father will not forgive us. That would not be good. If He cannot forgive us, He cannot hear us. He then asks the Father to lead us the right way and protect us from the evil one.

Many Christians pray for what they want and then wait to see what happens. I personally don't think we should pray like that. It's not about us. It's about God. He is the King and we are the servants. We need to pray for what He wants.

> *"This is the confidence we have in approaching God: that if we ask anything according to his will, he hears us. And if we know that he hears us—whatever we ask—we know that we have what we asked of him"*
> *(1 John 5:14-15).*

I don't want to waste my time praying for something God doesn't want or something I am not sure He wants. I'm not sure God wants me to have a red sports car or a bigger house so I don't pray for that. I have not seen anything in His word that says "you must have a bigger house and a red sports car. I command it". God will give me what He wants to give me and I will not argue with it. If He wants to give me, as my son says, a "ginormous" house, great! That will please God and it will please me too.

God tells us not to worry about tomorrow.

*"Therefore do not worry about tomorrow,
for tomorrow will worry about itself.
Each day has enough trouble of its own"
(Matthew 6:34).*

> God says the most important commandments are to love Him and our neighbor

I do believe God wants us to plan for the future. He just doesn't want us to worry about it. Here is some scripture on plans:

*"Plans fail for lack of counsel, but
with many advisers they succeed"
(Proverbs 15:22).*

*"Commit to the LORD whatever
you do, and your plans will succeed"
(Proverbs 16:3).*

*"In his heart a man plans his course,
but the LORD determines his steps"
(Proverbs 16:9).*

This is great. Now we know how to pray and what to do in order to have our plans succeed.

God asks us to forgive. If we forgive, we know we are forgiven. This gives us confidence before God.

*"But if you do not forgive men their sins,
your Father will not forgive your sins"
(Matthew 6:15).*

"Dear friends, if our hearts do not condemn

I know that if I pray for what God wants, I will receive what I ask

> *us, we have confidence before God and receive from him anything we ask, because we obey his commands and do what pleases him"*
> *(John 3:21-22).*

God says the most important commandments are to love Him and our neighbor.

> *"The most important one," answered Jesus, "is this: 'Hear, O Israel, the Lord our God, the Lord is one. Love the Lord your God with all your heart and with all your soul and with all your mind and with all your strength. 'The second is this: 'Love your neighbor as yourself. 'There is no commandment greater than these"*
> *(Mark 12:29-31).*

> *Love your brother so you won't stumble.*
> *(1 John 2:10)*

> *This is how we know what love is: Jesus Christ laid down his life for us. And we ought to lay down our lives for our brothers. If anyone has material possessions and sees his brother in need but has no pity on him, how can the love of God be in him? Dear children, let us not love with words or tongue but with actions and in truth.*
> *(1 John 3:16-18)*

If we do this, we please Him and everything else falls into place. It will also determine what we pray for.

I'm going to give an example of how I pray in regards to managing resources and why. Some people may disagree which frankly, is okay. I just want to give an example of how I think God wants me to pray.

The first thing I do is approach the throne in the name of Jesus. I praise and acknowledge Him. I forgive anyone who has wronged me and ask forgiveness for my sin.

"Though I have been speaking figuratively, a time is coming when I will no longer use this kind of language but will tell you plainly about my Father. In that day you will ask in my name. I am not saying that I will ask the Father on your behalf. No, the Father himself loves you because you have loved me and have believed that I came from God (John 16:25-27).

I know that if I pray for what God wants, I will receive what I ask. I know that God has a purpose for my life and a plan for me that will please Him. He has given me talents for His purpose.

I ask God to saturate my whole being with a desire for the purpose and vision He has for me. I ask Him to give me a hunger and an obsession for the purpose and tasks He has for me. I ask for increased wisdom and ability to perform the purpose He has for me. Then I ask for Him to order my steps and bring me together with the people He wants with me in order to accomplish what He wants. I commit these steps and every decision to Him so His plan will succeed.

I know God wants me to do the things He has for me to do. I know He wants me

> ...Jesus knew what His Father wanted

to accomplish the purpose He has for me. When I ask for this, I know I have it. Now I have to act on it. I know God is ordering my steps for His purpose.

> *"Therefore I tell you, whatever you ask for in prayer, believe that you have received it, and it will be yours"* (Mark 11:24).

There have been trials and everything does not always make sense, but I believe God's word.

> *"Consider it pure joy, my brothers, whenever you face trials of many kinds, because you know that the testing of your faith develops perseverance. Perseverance must finish its work so that you may be mature and complete, not lacking anything"* (James 1:2-4).

When I pray for the things mentioned earlier, I do not ask God if it is His will because I know it is His will. I know God wants me to do what He wills for my life. Some people attach the phrase "if it be your will" to everything they pray. I want to discuss how I view the following passages.

> *Going a little farther, he fell with his face to the ground and prayed, "My Father, if it is possible, may this cup be taken from me. Yet not as I will, but as you will"* (Matthew 26:39).

> *He went away a second time and prayed, "My Father, if it is not possible for this cup to be taken*

away unless I drink it, may your will be done"
(Matthew 26:42).

Jesus knew what the plan was. He had told His disciples many times what was going to happen. He was asking His Father if there was any other way within His will to accomplish what needed to be done. It appears to me that when Jesus went away a second time, He had received the same answer He had when He was sent to the world. The plan was not going to be changed. He told His Father, He would do it the way His Father wanted it done.

I cannot think of an example where two people are arguing but do not want something

"Put your sword back in its place," Jesus said to him, "for all who draw the sword will die by the sword. Do you think I cannot call on my Father, and he will at once put at my disposal more than twelve legions of angels? But how then would the Scriptures be fulfilled that say it must happen in this way?"
(Matthew 26:52-54)

The preceding passage indicates that Jesus knew what His Father wanted. His prayers demonstrated that He was human as well as He was God.

The following passage also addresses God's will.

"Now listen, you who say, 'Today or tomorrow we will go to this or that city, spend a year there, carry on business and make money.' Why, you do not even know what will happen tomorrow. What is your life? You are a mist that appears for a little while and then vanishes. Instead, you ought

> *to say, 'If it is the Lord's will, we will live and do this or that.' As it is, you boast and brag. All such boasting is evil. Anyone, then, who knows the good he ought to do and doesn't do it, sins (James 4:13-17).*

First of all, this is not a prayer and positive thinking is not faith. James is rebuking people who are bragging about what they are going to do even though they have no idea if it is what God wants. Instead we should tell people we want what God plans for us. James chapter four tells us that we fight and quarrel because we do not get what we want. I cannot think of an example where two people are arguing but do not want something. We will not receive if we do not ask for what God wants. Moreover, when we ask with our own selfish motives instead of God's motives, we will not receive what we ask. I believe we should ask God to cause us to want what He wants.

James states that it is adulterous to have friendship with the world and friendship with the world is hatred toward God.

> *"Do not love the world or anything in the world. If anyone loves the world, the love of the Father is not in him" (1 John 2:15).*

It is important to make sure we are not praying in accordance with worldly desires. This is often easier said than done. There are many prayers we can extract directly from the Word of God. When we do this, not only do we know we are praying according to God's will, we know we have what we are asking. As I study God's Word, I am constantly looking for things He wants me to ask Him for. When I see them, I pray them. Here are some examples.

> Yet, just because they cannot understand all that I tell them, it doesn't mean that I'm lying.

"For this reason, since the day we heard about you, we have not stopped praying for you and asking God to fill you with the knowledge of his will through all spiritual wisdom and understanding. And we pray this in order that you may live a life worthy of the Lord and may please him in every way: bearing fruit in every good work, growing in the knowledge of God, being strengthened with all power according to his glorious might so that you may have great endurance and patience, and joyfully giving thanks to the Father, who has qualified you to share in the inheritance of the saints in the kingdom of light" (Colossians 1:9-12).

". . . have not stopped giving thanks for you, remembering you in my prayers. I keep asking that the God of our Lord Jesus Christ, the glorious Father, may give you the Spirit of wisdom and revelation, so that you may know him better. I pray also that the eyes of your heart may be enlightened in order that you may know the hope to which he has called you, the riches of his glorious inheritance in the saints, and his incomparably great power for us who believe. That power is like the working of his mighty strength, which he exerted in Christ when he raised him from the dead and seated him at his right hand in the heavenly realms, far above all rule and authority, power and

> The way I see it, the problem is that my flesh and brain often get in the way of what my spirit knows

dominion, and every title that can be given, not only in the present age but also in the one to come" (Ephesians 1:16-21).

"For this reason I kneel before the Father, from whom his whole family in heaven and on earth derives its name. I pray that out of his glorious riches he may strengthen you with power through his Spirit in your inner being, so that Christ may dwell in your hearts through faith. And I pray that you, being rooted and established in love, may have power, together with all the saints, to grasp how wide and long and high and deep is the love of Christ, and to know this love that surpasses knowledge—that you may be filled to the measure of all the fullness of God" (Ephesians 3:14-19).

"Now to him who is able to do immeasurably more than all we ask or imagine, according to his power that is at work within us, to him be glory in the church and in Christ Jesus throughout all generations, forever and ever! Amen" (Ephesians 3:20-21).

"Search me, O God, and know my heart; test me and know my anxious thoughts. See if there is any offensive way in me, and lead me in the way everlasting" (Psalm 139:23-24).

Reading the Word of God and praying should be engaging. We should be engaging God. When we pray, we should not just be talking. If I'm having a conversation with God, it's wiser to listen than it is to talk.

GOD'S DIMENSIONS

My children are young. They cannot understand everything I tell them or teach them. Yet, just because they cannot understand all that I tell them, it doesn't mean that I'm lying. Just because what I say to them might not make sense to them, it does not mean what I say is not true. I know what God says is true. I just do not always understand it.

Jesus said the Father will send us the Holy Spirit to teach us. All we have to do is ask.

*"But the Counselor, the Holy Spirit,
whom the Father will send in my name,
will teach you all things and will remind
you of everything I have said to you"
(John 14:26).*

...time does not exist in heaven

Wow! Because I have received Christ and have His Spirit, the preceding verse suggests that the Spirit of God is teaching me.

*"If you then, though you are evil, know
how to give good gifts to your children,
how much more will your Father in heaven
give the Holy Spirit to those who ask him!"
(Luke 11:13)*

The way I see it, the problem is that my flesh and brain often get in the way of what my spirit knows.

> *"We have not received the spirit of the world but the Spirit who is from God, that we may understand what God has freely given us. This is what we speak, not in words taught us by human wisdom but in words taught by the Spirit, expressing spiritual truths in spiritual words"*
> *(1 Corinthians 2:12-13).*

> *"The Spirit gives life; the flesh counts for nothing. The words I have spoken to you are spirit and they are life"*
> *(John 6:63).*

I'm going to guess the people who have crucified their flesh the most and moved toward the Spirit of God are the ones who are hearing what God is teaching the most.

There are two parts to us. One part is spiritual and the other is physical. We are spiritual beings, yet we operate in the physical realm that we know as the world.

We operate in and understand some of the dimensions of our world. We do not know how many dimensions or understand the spiritual dimensions of God. If we add or subtract just one dimension from our world, it would throw us into a tail spin. God operates on a different dimension. God operates in the spirit realm.

Physics: The science that deals with and force.
(http://dictionary.reference.com/browse/physics)

A number of years ago I was driving over to say good-bye to my father-in-law who was on his death bed. On my way over, God showed me something that I often think about. I repeated it to my father-in-law when I arrived.

> What is a stay at home mom's labor worth?

God is the beginning and the end. He always was and always will be. This is no great revelation to believers of the Bible. However; if you think about this on a deep level, it can put some serious stress on your brain.

This means time does not exist in heaven. This is hard to wrap our minds around because we operate in our world which has a time dimension.

What would it be like if there was no time? We would not have to wait for anything. Waiting would not even be possible. When my father-in-law entered heaven, he did not have to wait for other loved ones to join him. They are already there because time does not exist.

I'm not trying to freak people out. My point is that we do not always know what's best for us because we don't know everything that God knows. God operates in dimensions we don't completely understand. He knows the future. Our flesh gets in the way of full understanding.

Now we see but a poor reflection as in a mirror; then we shall see face to face. Now I know in part;

then I shall know fully, even as I am fully known.
(1 Cor 13:12)

THE VALUE OF LABOR

How is the value of labor determined? Before money, people bartered. A farmer who grew corn would trade his corn for beef with a rancher. Each applied their labor in order to produce their products. A blacksmith would trade horseshoes for fur with a trapper.

If we do not trust our pastor with our money, we should go to a different church

There were some problems with this barter system. What if the rancher only needed ten ears of corn? Would he give the farmer a whole cow? What if the rancher also wanted apples, but the first farmer only had corn? It was difficult to determine how many ears of corn were equal to a cow. It was easier to put a money value on each item. Money could be in the form of paper or poker-chips. The bottom line was that something was needed to represent the farmer's labor which had been stored in the form of corn: Money. Money represents products produced by labor. Now the rancher could determine what value he was willing to pay for an ear of corn and what value he would place on a cow.

Supply and demand affects the value of each item. If it takes skilled labor to produce a product in limited supply but in great demand, the value will be high. This same reality occurs for services provided.

HOME MAKER

My wife is a stay at home mom. She is incredibly gifted. She can do things that I cannot and always seems to be more talented than I am. I'm not wired like my wife. What is a stay at home mom's labor worth? I have seen statistics that say it is worth about $120,000 per year. The work week is approximately ninety-five hours per week.

It is hard to put a value on this, but I'll try. Both of our children are in their early school years. My wife spends many quality hours with each of our children every day. A value cannot be put on this effort. She is teaching them biblical principles and values. As our kids grow, these values will have an impact for God. The positive impact my wife has on our children cannot be measured. When I think of the impact our children will have on others, my wife's labor is multiplied exponentially for God. In this light it's easy to see how touching one life can make a significant difference.

> Pastors don't have to be reminded that they have taken on a very serious responsibility

I often care for our kids while Laura takes short overnight or weekend trips with her sister or her friends. Every time I do this, it reminds me how amazing the talents that God has given my wife truly are.

PASTOR

A Godly pastor meets the requirements and has the gifts laid out in the Word of God. A gifted pastor is also a good leader. Leading is not carried out by hand holding or telling others what to do. In my view, a great pastor creates a platform where the vision God has given him can thrive. This platform should have enough flexibility to allow the Spirit of God to move. It also allows individuals to use the gifts and talents God has given them within the vision given to the pastor. This is great leadership and creates disciples for Christ. The pastors who have spiritual authority over me are experts at this.

I must point out before getting into the value of a Pastor's labor that I have not been put up to this by any of my Pastors or Pastor Friends. I have not discussed my thoughts on this with any Pastors, so that they cannot be blamed for what I think. What is a Godly Pastor's labor worth? I have been in the church since I was a young boy. I have noticed that many church members often put their pastor up on a pedestal then suck the life out of them and their families. They are expected to be perfect, yet the truth is they are not. The pressures and expectations put on Pastors by church members are great. The responsibility of a pastor is great. What is the value of a pastor's labor? What is their value to God?

> There is a debate in the church about whether God wants people to be rich

There are CEOs (Chief Executive Officers) of many publicly held companies that earn tens of millions even hundreds of millions of dollars per year. Most executives of large publicly held companies earn millions of dollars per year. It seems to me that not only do church members suck the life out of their pastors but they assume the value of a pastor's labor is very little. Without painting all church goers with the same brush stroke, it seems that people expect pastors to be paid in peanuts. I don't think this is how God views it. Is the value of a Pastor doing God's will higher than a CEO? What does God think?

Money is labor. Our pastors work for God and serve us. We should pay them well because that is what I believe God wants. When we pay our pastors with our money, we are paying them in labor. If we do not trust our pastor with our money, we should go to a different church. Pastors connected to God who are performing His will are capable of managing millions of dollars for Him. Their personal paychecks as a result should be high.

In addition to the tithe, I want to encourage church members to pay the pastors of their local church through an offering. I don't do this at my local church only because it discourages most offering earmarks. They have a valid reason for discouraging this that has to do with their stewardship of tithes and offerings. However many churches do permit this. This special offering is always above the usual tithe.

Pastors don't have to be reminded that they have taken on a very serious responsibility. I have joked with some of my pastors that I'm going to blame all my faults on them.

MISSIONARY

God has called all believers in Christ to be real rich but not all believers to be fake rich

"Then Jesus told them this parable: "Suppose one of you has a hundred sheep and loses one of them. Does he not leave the ninety-nine in the open country and go after the lost sheep until he finds it? And when he finds it, he joyfully puts it on his shoulders and goes home. Then he calls his friends and neighbors together and says, 'Rejoice with me; I have found my lost sheep.' I tell you that in the same way there will be more rejoicing in heaven over one sinner who repents than over ninety-nine righteous persons who do not need to repent" (Luke 15:3-7).

Angels rejoice when a soul is saved. What value does God put on a missionary's labor? What true riches are they storing in heaven? In the parable of the talents God is expressing His desire for us to increase them. When a missionary leads someone to Christ and helps them become a disciple, his or her talents are increased. This is true wealth.

THE GREAT COMMISSION

If we are committed to Christ, our time and labor is committed to Christ. What this means is that the money which God has put under our management is committed to Christ. Jesus said:

> *"All authority in heaven and on earth has been given to me. Therefore go and make disciples of all nations, baptizing them in the name of the Father and of the Son and of the Holy Spirit, and teaching them to obey everything I have commanded you. And surely I am with you always, to the very end of the age."*
> *(Matthew 28:18-20)*

Clearly, God doesn't want us to serve money or put our trust in money

This is what Jesus wants us to do with the resources He has put under our management. This includes our resources in the form of labor, time, talents, and money.

RICH VS. POOR

"No servant can serve two masters. Either he will hate the one and love the other, or he will be devoted to the one and despise the other. You cannot serve both God and Money."

The Pharisees, who loved money, heard all this and were sneering at Jesus. He said to them, "You are the ones who justify yourselves in the eyes of men, but God knows your hearts. What is highly valued among men is detestable in God's sight"
(Luke 16:13-15).

There is a debate in the church about whether God wants people to be rich. Some say it is our right as believers in Christ to accumulate great wealth. If we pick and choose individual passages from the Word of God, it is easy

> Every purchase I make, whether it's a product or service should glorify God first

to argue this one way or another. People get caught up on the terms others use when trying to communicate. Then they pick apart the terms. My approach to analyzing this is different. I try to focus on what God wants and what He is saying. People nit-picking over terms are often saying the same thing. When we focus on God's priorities, it's much easier to determine how much money God wants us to have. We can determine if God wants us to be rich and whether or not it's a right as a believer in Christ. The big question is what is rich? There are probably hundreds of views.

I discussed the rich man in Mark chapter 10. Jesus said it is harder for a rich man to enter the Kingdom of God than it is for a camel to go through the eye of a needle. I want to evaluate this rich man in Mark chapter 10. The same account is described in Matthew 19:1630 and Luke 18:1830. If you really want to analyze this I would recommend reading all the accounts in multiple versions of the bible and even in the Greek language. This is my perception. I wonder how rich this man was. I don't know what he had or thought he had, but I do know some things he did not have. Here is a list of what he did not have.

- Dish washer

- Washer and Dryer

- Air conditioning

- Gas heat

- Electricity

- Cell phone

- Microwave oven

- Running water

- Sports car

- IPod

- MP3 player

- Computer High definition

- Plasma television

- Digital surround sound

- Sport Utility Vehicle (SUV)

- Any type of phone at all

I could go on with this list. Many people reading this book have most of the stuff that I've listed. Stuff is nothing. This rich man described in the Bible had nothing real and He had very little of the fake riches most Americans have today. I believe the Bible is talking about two kinds of rich when it talks about money, that being fake rich and real rich. Fake rich is stuff on earth. This fake rich stuff can and should be managed for God's purpose. Real rich, on the other hand is what we are building in heaven. We can and should use fake rich to build real

> God talks and whatever He wants to occur happens

rich in heaven. God has called all believers in Christ to be real rich but not all believers to be fake rich.

In 1 Timothy 6:17-19, Paul is addressing those who are rich in this present world. People who are rich in this present world are managing fake riches which are real resources for God. We need to increase them for God's purpose. We just don't own them.

> *"Command those who are rich in this present world not to be arrogant nor to put their hope in wealth, which is so uncertain, but to put their hope in God, who richly provides us with everything for our enjoyment. Command them to do good, to be rich in good deeds, and to be generous and willing to share. In this way they will lay up treasure for themselves as a firm foundation for the coming age, so that they may take hold of the life that is truly life"*
> *(1 Timothy 6:17-19).*

It seems to me that Paul was talking to Christians who are rich in this present world. This means it must be possible for people with significant amounts of money on earth to go to heaven. However, this present world is temporal. If worldly riches are temporary, that means people with riches in this present world do not get to keep those riches. That's a no-brainer. We don't get to haul our stuff into the afterlife. If we don't get to keep the riches, we don't own the riches. We are just managing the riches. Yes, God wants those talents to grow for His purpose. I believe God wants us to enjoy what he provides for us on earth. Once again, motive is the key.

So who are these rich people who will have a more difficult time inheriting the Kingdom of God than it is for a camel to go through the eye of a needle? I have known many people with over ten million dollars, but these people didn't consider themselves to be rich. If I handed most people five million dollars they would immediately consider themselves rich in worldly terms. This then begs the question, who is rich? This is how dictionary.com defines rich:

"Having wealth or great possessions; abundantly supplied with resources, means, or funds."

Let's compare the average person living in the United States with the rich man Jesus met. The average United States citizen has far more wealth and luxury at their fingertips than the rich man in Mark chapter 10. Does that mean it's impossible for the average American to enter the Kingdom of God? The answer is no. Anyone who chooses to put their trust in God rather than stuff can be saved. As I mentioned in the chapter called "One Master", it's about how we look at our stuff. Do we serve God or money? We cannot serve both. This means we cannot serve even a small amount of money. People can serve small amounts of money just like they can serve large amounts of money.

Clearly, God doesn't want us to serve money or put our trust in money. He doesn't want

> I also pray that God will not allow us to manage more than we can handle, but as much as we can handle

> When the disciples acted on their faith by passing out the bread Jesus gave them, it increased

us to put our trust in anything other than Him. Now for my explanation to the big question as I see it: Does God want us to be rich? God's first priority is our spiritual health and our relationship with Him. God only gives us good gifts. He isn't going to give us something that will jeopardize our relationship with Him or the real riches that He has for us. He wants us to be rich toward Him and put our treasures in heaven. God wants us to serve Him. When we labor for God, we serve Him. Money can be converted to labor or products. Every purchase I make, whether it's a product or service should glorify God first. If it's a home, an automobile, a swimming pool, or a chair, it should be for God first and His purpose.

God has commanded us to take part in the great commission. That means we are to apply our labor toward the great commission. The more labor we have under management, the greater our impact will be. Money is labor. I believe God wants us to have the maximum amount of labor/money under our management that we can handle. I say, God wants to maximize the labor under His servants' management. This is contingent on the notion that money will not bring ruin. God's servants must realize they don't own anything and they must not put their trust in money. If money is an idol, God is not first. God does not want to share us with an idol. He is a jealous God. We must avoid the temptation of becoming secure because of the wealth under our management.

"Break down their altars, smash their sacred stones and cut down their Asherah poles. Do not worship any other god, for the LORD, whose name is Jealous, is a jealous God".

"Be careful not to make a treaty with those who live in the land; for when they prostitute themselves to their gods and sacrifice to them, they will invite you and you will eat their sacrifices" (Exodus 34:13-15).

I believe it's important to surround ourselves with Godly people who can help us to be accountable in managing money. This will also help us avoid the influence of people worshiping idols. I also pray that God will not allow us to manage more than we can handle, but as much as we can handle.

I always try to remember God wants us to be rich but he wants us to be rich with what I believe are real riches.

And he told them this parable: "The ground of a certain rich man produced a good crop. He thought to himself, 'What shall I do? I have no place to store my crops.'

"Then he said, 'This is what I'll do. I will tear down my barns and build bigger ones, and there I will store all my grain and my goods. And I'll say to myself, "You have plenty of good things laid up for many years. Take life easy; eat, drink and be merry."

"But God said to him, 'You fool! This very night your life will be demanded from you. Then who

> *will get what you have prepared for yourself?'*
>
> *"This is how it will be with anyone who stores up things for himself but is not rich toward God."*
> *(Luke 12:16-21)*

Some people are far richer than it appears. Others by comparison are flat broke when they are rich in worldly possessions. God can multiply our labor with His math just like He can multiply a fish. When we use our labor to serve God, He can multiply those riches far beyond what meets the eye.

REST IN THE LORD

"All In" is a term used in poker. It means you are putting all you have in the pot because you believe you have the best hand. Jesus is our hand. We have the best hand. There is nothing that can beat our hand.

I want to be "All In" for Jesus. That means I am betting everything on Jesus and holding nothing back. That means not one chip is held back. That is my prayer.

> *And God said, "Let there be light," and there was light. God saw that the light was good, and he separated the light from the darkness. God called the light "day," and the darkness he called "night." And there was evening, and there was morning — the first day.*

And God said, "Let there be an expanse between the waters to separate water from water." So God made the expanse and separated the water under the expanse from the water above it. And it was so. God called the expanse "sky." And there was evening, and there was morning — the second day.

And God said, "Let the water under the sky be gathered to one place, and let dry ground appear." And it was so. God called the dry ground "land," and the gathered waters he called "seas." And God saw that it was good (Genesis 1:3-10).

Let this passage sink into your spirit. God said "let there be light". God talks and whatever He wants to occur happens. Why do we so often put Him in a box and hesitate to trust Him?

"But remember the Lord your God, for it is he who gives you the ability to produce wealth, and so confirms his covenant, which he swore to your forefathers, as it is today" (Deuteronomy 8:18).

God is in control. Let us just rest in Him and let go of our worries and fears.

"Commit to the Lord whatever you do, and your plans will succeed" (Proverbs 16:3).

When we rest in the Lord, it brings to us a sense of peace and has a calming effect on us. The Word of God gives us so many examples and demonstrates that God will more than meet our needs.

"The Pharisees came and began to question Jesus. To test him, they asked him for a sign from heaven. He sighed deeply and said, "Why does this generation ask for a miraculous sign? I tell you the truth, no sign will be given to it." Then he left them, got back into the boat and crossed to the other side.

The disciples had forgotten to bring bread, except for one loaf they had with them in the boat. "Be careful," Jesus warned them. "Watch out for the yeast of the Pharisees and that of Herod."

They discussed this with one another and said, "It is because we have no bread."

Aware of their discussion, Jesus asked them: "Why are you talking about having no bread? Do you still not see or understand? Are your hearts hardened? Do you have eyes but fail to see, and ears but fail to hear? And don't you remember? When I broke the five loaves for the five thousand, how many basketfuls of pieces did you pick up?"

"Twelve," they replied.

"And when I broke the seven loaves for the four thousand, how many basketfuls of pieces did you pick up?"

They answered, "Seven."

He said to them, "Do you still not understand?"
(Mark 8:11-21)

Notice in the previous passage that the Pharisees wanted to see proof before they would believe Jesus. That's not how it works. Remember Hebrews 11:1? Faith is the proof of what we don't see.

The disciples of Jesus were looking at their physical circumstance realizing that they forgot to bring more than one loaf of bread. Jesus was talking about the teachings of the Pharisees. Just like the disciples, we often don't use our faith to see truth.

When the disciples acted on their faith by passing out the bread Jesus gave them, it increased. While they didn't know exactly how much bread they really had, they knew they had more than enough. Notice that when five loaves were broken for five thousand, twelve basketfuls of pieces were picked up. When seven loaves were broken for four thousand, there were seven basketfuls of pieces picked up. When faith was acted on, the amount of bread was seen.

What would have happened if the disciples would have just stood there with the bread? The answer is nothing. They would have been standing there with much too little to feed thousands of people. If they would have held onto it long enough it would have spoiled.

When we trust God and put our confidence in Him, we will be blessed.

This is what the Lord says:

> *"Cursed is the one who trusts in man, who depends on flesh for his strength and whose heart turns away from the Lord. He will be like a bush in the wastelands; he will not see prosperity when it comes. He will dwell in the parched places of the desert, in a salt land where no one lives.*
>
> *"But blessed is the man who trusts in the Lord, whose confidence is in him. He will be like a tree planted by the water that sends out its roots by the stream. It does not fear when heat comes; its leaves are always green. It has no worries in a year of drought and never fails to bear fruit."*
> *(Jeremiah 17:5-8)*

I believe it is wiser to trust God than to trust stuff. When we put our trust in God and act on it, we will not fear job loss, recession, depression, or anything else. We will always bear fruit for our Lord and Savior.

www.ingramcontent.com/pod-product-compliance
Lightning Source LLC
Chambersburg PA
CBHW061657040426
42446CB00010B/1783